OLD FAITHFUL ERUPTS AT SUNDOWN IN A SNOW-COATED GEYSER FIELD IN YELLOWSTONE

YELLOWSTONE

www.nationalgeographic.com

Printed in China

23/RRDH/12

Composition for this book by the Typographic section of National Geographic Production Services, Pre-Press Division. Printed and bound by R. R. Donnelley & Sons, Willard, Ohio. Color separations by Graphic Art Service, Inc., Nashville, Tenn.; Lanman Progressive Company, Washington, D.C.; and Lincoln Graphics, Inc., Cherry Hill, N.J.

Library of Congress ℗ Data
Fishbein, Seymour L.
  Yellowstone country; the enduring wonder/by Seymour L. Fishbein; photographed by Raymond Gehman.
  p. cm.
  "Prepared by the Book Division, National Geographic Society, Washington, D.C."
  Bibliography: p.
  Includes index.
  ISBN 0-87044-713-0 (regular edition)
  ISBN 0-87044-718-1 (library edition)
  1. Yellowstone National Park. 2. Ecology – Yellowstone National Park. 3. Grand Teton National Park (Wyo.). 4. Ecology – Wyoming – Grand Teton National Park. I. National Geographic Society (U.S.). Books Division. II. Title
F722.F57 1989
917.87'526dc20   89-3353
                                        CIP

Index

Acknowledgments

Raymond Gehman dedicates his photographs in this book to the memory of his father, Earl W. Gehman.

The Special Publications Division is grateful to the individuals named or quoted in the text and to those cited here for their assistance during the production of this book: Don Cushman, John Daugherty, Edna Good, and Patrick Smith of Grand Teton National Park; Joan Anzelmo, Norman Bishop, Mary Anne Davis, Don Despain, Ron Jones, Greg Kroll, Tim Manns, Mark Marschall, Mike Pflaum, Sandi Robinson, Frank Singer, Jim Sweaney, and Amy Vanderbilt of Yellowstone National Park; John Wilbrecht and James Griffin of the National Elk Refuge; the staffs of Bridger-Teton National Forest, Custer N.F., Gallatin N.F., Shoshone N.F., and Targhee N.F.; and the staffs of Grays Lake National Wildlife Refuge and Red Rock Lakes National Wildlife Refuge.

We also thank the following people for so generously sharing their experience and expertise with us: Drew Barney; Robert Christiansen and Dan Dzurisin of the U.S. Geological Survey; Marilyn J. Collins of the Bureau of Reclamation; M. Lynne Corn and Ross W. Gorte of the Congressional Research Service; Shirley Coulston; Richard Crosman; Doug Edgerton; Hank Fischer of Defenders of Wildlife; Barry Flamm of the Wilderness Society; James P. Foley, Jr.; Steven Fuller; Carrie Hunt; Charles Kay of Utah State University; Clayton Marlow and Dave Ward of Montana State University; Leigh Ortenburger; Richard Parks; Larry Roop of the Wyoming Game and Fish Department; Meredith and Tory Taylor; Jack Troyer of the Greater Yellowstone Coordinating Committee; Jack Turnell; Louisa Willcox, Todd Wilkinson, and Ed Lewis of the Greater Yellowstone Coalition; John Weaver of the U.S. Forest Service; and John Winsor.

Additional Reading

The reader may wish to consult the *National Geographic Index* for related articles and books. We also found the following books particularly helpful: Orville E. Bach, Jr., *Hiking the Yellowstone Backcountry*; Richard A. Bartlett, *Yellowstone: A Wilderness Besieged* and *Nature's Yellowstone*; Robert B. Betts, *Along the Ramparts of the Tetons: The Saga of Jackson Hole, Wyoming*; Orrin H. and Lorraine G. Bonney, *Guide to the Wyoming Mountains and Wilderness Areas*; Nathaniel Burt, *Jackson Hole Journal*; Alston Chase, *Playing God In Yellowstone: The Destruction of America's First National Park*; Hiram Martin Chittenden, *The Yellowstone National Park*; Frank C. Craighead, Jr., *Track of the Grizzly*; John J. Craighead et al., *A Field Guide to Rocky Mountain Wildflowers*; Don Despain *et al.*, *Wildlife in Transition: Man and Nature on Yellowstone's Northern Range*; William J. Fritz, *Roadside Geology of the Yellowstone Country*; Fritiof Fryxell, *The Tetons: Interpretations of a Mountain Landscape*; Aubrey L. Haines, *The Yellowstone Story*; Stephen Herrero, *Bear Attacks: Their Causes and Avoidance*; William R. Keefer, *The Geologic Story of Yellowstone National Park*; Joe Kelsey, *Climbing and Hiking in the Wind River Mountains*; Dean Krakel II, *Season of the Elk*; Nathaniel Pitt Langford, *The Discovery of Yellowstone Park 1870*; J. D. Love and John C. Reed, *Creation of the Teton Landscape*; Thomas McNamee, *The Grizzly Bear*; Margaret and Olaus Murie, *Wapiti Wilderness*; Leigh Ortenburger, *A Climber's Guide to the Teton Range*; Rick Reese, *Greater Yellowstone: The National Park and Adjacent Wildlands*; Robert W. Righter, *Crucible for Conservation: The Creation of Grand Teton National Park*; Osborne Russell, *Journal of a Trapper [1834-1843]*; Carl Schreier, *Yellowstone Explorers Guide*; Paul Schullery, *The Bears of Yellowstone* and ed., *Old Yellowstone Days*.

*A*lert to a nearby noise, a bull moose near the Snake River looks warily around. Mild winters in recent years helped assure plenty of forage for growing numbers of animals in Yellowstone country. Drought and the fires of 1988 brought scarcity; unusually high numbers of animals starved, or, beyond park boundaries, were shot during the winter of '88-89. Conservation groups and the National Park Service agree on the need for additional winter range, particularly for bison and elk.

hot chocolate and soups into him, warming his feet. For more than an hour, all he could say in response to our questioning was, "My feet feel like clay." Then a bit of feeling returned, and he fell into sleep.

The night was long and cold, perhaps 30 below. Though we saw little sign of snow, warmer air had clearly moved in. By morning Rick had feeling in his feet and pain in his knee. Stan Beafore, summoned by radio, skied up with a litter, and Rick was eased down. I learned later that he suffered no permanent injury.

Yellowstone is harsh country. Small emergencies may command large energies, skill, and caring. All were in evidence on the frozen slopes of Dunraven. I felt privileged to witness it.

Down from Dunraven, I caught a ride back to the Snow Lodge at Old Faithful on one of the snowcoaches grinding around the Grand Loop with tourists. Bison peppered the gray-white hills of Hayden Valley. Dark-hued little ducks dabbled in the Yellowstone River, workaday drones overshadowed by the slow-moving trumpeters, majestic in size and bearing. A coyote in the road held its ground before us for a time, then slowly turned off into the wood, with a look askance at the abominable snow machine.

There are other sideways glances at the winter crowd. Its "phenomenal" growth, observed then National Park Service Director William Penn Mott in the spring of 1987, had not been accompanied by increased funding, stretching thin the small winter staff. Some wonder at the impact on wildlife, the roar of motors in the winter hush. Others say they have seen little damage brought on by the influx.

No harm to Yellowstone, no harm to the ecosystem. I heard that refrain in park and forest, in town and mine and sawmill, from the east side of the Beartooths to the west side of the Tetons, from the Gallatins in the northwest to the Wind Rivers in the southeast. That is the promise made by proponents of park developments and of timbering and mining and energy exploration and ski resorts and subdivisions in the forests. Taken individually, some developments may indeed do no harm. But the cumulative impact, warn environmental groups, may "irreversibly degrade this unique national treasure."

On my last winter morning in Yellowstone a fickle breeze nipped around. At 8:20 the most renowned of geysers went off: seeping water, superheated in some conjectured caldron deep in the earth, which no one had ever seen, boiling up out of the spine of the continent, where the temperature at this moment stood at 12 below zero.

From behind the eastern ridge the unseen sun caught the surging plume and mellowed it. Wind near the ground bent it northward, then a variant wind curled the gleaming steam cloud around to the southwest. It seemed to me that Old Faithful was skywriting, and what it wrote was a giant, ragged question mark that gradually blurred as it drifted off, across the sintery hill, across the cold lava ridges, across the enduring wonderland that is Yellowstone country.

FOLLOWING PAGES: Shaft of early morning light showers a pine standing sentry above the Grand Canyon of the Yellowstone River; frost, formed as thermal steam rises and freezes, forms a shimmering halo. Snow dapples jagged canyon walls of yellow rhyolite lava. In the grand mosaic of Greater Yellowstone— a kaleidoscope of wonders— each scene shifts as the seasons turn.

STEVEN FULLER (FOLLOWING PAGES)

edged close. When the otters moved against the intruder, another raven swooped down and flapped off with the unguarded fish. Naturalist Roger Anderson watched this. Then something went amiss. One day Roger discovered black feathers and blood on the ice. A surviving raven came around, a black fury, and dive-bombed the enemy, to no effect. Quoth the otter: "Nevermore."

At Canyon Village one day Mary McCutcheon noted a temperature of minus 30°F; but she had seen it as low as minus 42, so 30 below could hardly be called extreme. The next morning I was drinking tea with her husband, Mark, at their dining table. He was the head ranger at Canyon, and, as usual, had his park radio on. At 8 a.m. Mark's assistant Stan Beafore radioed a reading from a field thermometer a few hundred yards away— "minus 42." In a few minutes Stan knocked on the door, ogled the tea, and sat down with a cup. His lungs had burned a little when he set out on patrol, but otherwise nothing bothered. "I had to extrapolate," he reported to Mark. "That thing was off the charts." The lowest minus number on the field thermometer was 40.

As we dressed, the stereo set a cheery note with a tune from the musical "Fiddler on the Roof," the old Hebrew toast, *"L'Chaim*—To Life." Even more appropriate would be what accompanied that toast in the days of my growing up: a finger or two of what we called schnapps, urban moonshine, an amber lightning that put fire in the belly.

This was the day we were going camping, Mark's weekly night out with Yellowstone rangers—for winter survival training in snow shelters on the slopes of Dunraven Peak, above 9,000 feet, a thousand feet higher than where the thermometer ran out of numbers. Not to worry. We were due for snow. Snow up here means warmer air; it would drive out the sink of cold air that had settled in.

By the time we left, in midmorning, the temperature had soared to 25 below. Even without a snowstorm. At road's end we shouldered packs and skied for about two miles, the final stretch switchbacking up Dunraven, in the Washburn Range. At the site, on a snow slope angled toward the sun, Mark dug a couch-potato hollow. Into this solarium we flopped and basked, letting the sweat dry in the midday sun.

In the afternoon the rangers dug snow shelters and learned avalanche rescue, searching with radios and with long poles probing into the deep snow. Toward day's end some had enough energy left to do a little telemarking, cutting elegant curves around pristine snow dunes, ripples of light and shadow.

Mark and I shared a commodious igloo left over from a previous exercise. The snow bricks were translucent at the joints, providing ribbons of indirect lighting. As we melted snow on the pack stove, Ranger Rick Anderson crawled through the entryway and announced, "I have no feeling in my feet." Rick had sweated hard while digging a shelter. He had fallen in deep snow and wrenched a knee. Then hypothermia set in. We thawed him inside and out, spooning

That same winter, an employee at the Snow Lodge went camping at Shoshone Lake. At night, in a driving snowstorm, he fell into a hot spring with a temperature of 182°F. He dragged himself out and made it back to camp. His companions set out through the dark, storm-wracked wilderness to summon help at Old Faithful, 9.5 miles away. He lay in agony for 12 hours before he died.

Snowcoaches follow sections of the Grand Loop, covering 200 clanking miles soothed by the sight of the Grand Canyon, the Yellowstone River with its flotillas of waterfowl, and Norris and West Thumb Geyser Basins. Norris is the hottest, most violent of the basins. Each year, a widespread disturbance muddies the waters at Norris and throws the geyser schedules out of kilter. In 1986 little Porkchop Geyser—named for the shape of its pool—became a full-time spouter for three years, shooting a fine spray as high as 25 feet, with a roar that could be heard half a mile away. In winter the spray froze, sheathing downwind trees and building a giant loaf of blue ice. Once Rick Hutchinson figured the volume at 421 cubic meters, enough to make 13.4 million silica-rich ice cubes. There was nothing else like it in the park.

At West Thumb a family of otters had taken up residence. They made their living by fishing, diving for cutthroat trout just off the shore of Yellowstone Lake. Ravens plagued them with a sucker game. As the otters dined, a decoy raven

Shaggy coat caked with snow, a bison (right) forages near a thermal area. Well adapted to the park's harsh winters, bison "shelter" inside their thick hides. They simply bed down, sometimes in the lee of a hill. Most of Yellowstone's 3,500 bison survive the winter. The youngest, oldest, and weakest fall prey most often to extreme cold and hunger (opposite). Death forms a vital link in the park's food chain. Carcasses nourish coyotes, bears, ravens, and other scavengers.

Firehole dumped me every time. I headed for the trail to Lone Star Geyser, to the little hill where instructors from the ski shop give lessons and where incompetents do penance. Michael Shaik and I shared the hill. Nearby, at a bend in the Firehole, four elk scraped for food. A pine marten slinked across the snow.

In this sublime setting Michael and I rehearsed the comic gaits that help skiers negotiate hills and turns. Herring-bone and snowplow: Charlie Chaplin up the hill, Jerry Lewis down. With lots of pratfalls. Finally Michael had had enough. As he picked himself up, he scanned the conifer forest, weighted with snow. "Cor!" he exclaimed. "We never see anything like this except on Christmas cards." Certainly not at this time of year. Michael was on summer break. In March he began his second year at the University of Tasmania.

Whatever the skills, Yellowstone has trails to match, sights to see. One day I skied with Rick and Jen Hutchinson to Fairy Falls, which spills 200 feet down through a collar of blue ice against a wall of obsidian and rhyolite, frozen white. The air was alive with the whistling of mountain chickadees, the snow pocked with the deep tracks of elk, with the light prints of snowshoe hares. A bald eagle stared down from its lodgepole perch. Beside the trail lay a bison carcass, neat arcs of rib cages picked clean by coyotes. With nature's elegant timing, winter die-off of elk and bison reaches a peak in March and April, when the grizzlies, fresh from their dens, join the scavenging.

On another day I skied with naturalist Carl Schreier down the Upper Geyser Basin to Black Sand Geyser Basin and Biscuit Basin, past the gleaming pools of Artemisia, Sapphire, Emerald, and Morning Glory. The thermal waters keep meadows thawed and streams open, to the benefit of wildlife. But they can also kill. At Black Sand Pool a pair of goldeneyes had evidently tried to land on the boiling surface. The female managed to reach the pool's edge before expiring. The male floated in the pool, white belly up.

COUNTRY
The Enduring Wonder

By Seymour L. Fishbein
Photographed by Raymond Gehman

Prepared by the Book Division
National Geographic Society, Washington, D.C.

Yellowstone Country
The Enduring Wonder

By SEYMOUR L. FISHBEIN
Photographed by RAYMOND GEHMAN

Published by THE NATIONAL GEOGRAPHIC SOCIETY
REG MURPHY,
 President and Chief Executive Officer
GILBERT M. GROSVENOR,
 Chairman of the Board
NINA D. HOFFMAN, *Senior Vice President*

Prepared by The Book Division
WILLIAM R. GRAY, *Vice President and Director*
CHARLES KOGOD, *Assistant Director*
BARBARA A. PAYNE, *Editorial Director*

Staff for this Book
PAUL MARTIN, *Managing Editor*
TONI EUGENE, *Associate Managing Editor*
CHARLES KOGOD, *Illustrations Editor*
CINDA ROSE, *Art Director*
SALLIE M. GREENWOOD, ALISON KAHN,
 VALERIE A. MAY, Researchers
M. BARBARA BROWNELL, SEYMOUR L. FISHBEIN,
JANE R. MCCAULEY, THOMAS O'NEILL,
 CYNTHIA RUSS RAMSAY, JENNIFER C. URQUHART,
 Picture Legend Writers
JOHN D. GARST, JR., VIRGINIA L. BAZA,
 JUDITH F. BELL, ROBERT W. CRONAN,
 SVEN M. DOLLING, SUSAN I. FRIEDMAN,
 MARTIN S. WALTZ, *Map Production and Research*
SANDRA F. LOTTERMAN, *Editorial Assistant*
SHARON KOCSIS BERRY, *Illustrations Assistant*

Engraving, Printing, and Product Manufacture
GEORGE V. WHITE, *Director,* and
 VINCENT P. RYAN, *Manager, Manufacturing
 and Quality Management*
DAVID V. SHOWERS, *Production Manager*
KEVIN P. HEUBUSCH, *Production Project Manager*
LEWIS R. BASSFORD, *Assistant Production Manager*
KATHLEEN M. CIRUCCI, TIMOTHY H. EWING,
 Senior Production Assistants
CAROL R. CURTIS, *Senior Production Staff Assistant*
SUSAN A. BENDER, CATHERINE G. CRUZ,
 MARISA J. FARABELLI, KAREN KATZ,
 LISA A. LAFURIA, ELIZA MORTON,
 DRU STANCAMPIANO, *Staff Assistants*
BRYAN K. KNEDLER, *Indexer*

*Inching up a frozen snowdrift, a naturalist skirts
Yellowstone's Porkchop Geyser, which blew itself out of
existence in 1989.*
PRECEDING PAGES: *A bull elk bugles during the fall rut.*

*V*eiled in morning mist, the Yellowstone River winds through
Hayden Valley. Set between the Washburn Range and Yellowstone
Lake, the valley honors geologist Ferdinand Hayden, whose area
survey in 1871 helped inspire the creation of the world's first national park.

Foreword

By Frank C. Craighead, Jr.

Stepping off the running board of my Chevy onto the gravel road down Togwotee Pass, I caught my breath at the jagged Tetons—my first sight of them. It was 1935, six years after the creation of Grand Teton National Park. To the north the land sloped up to the earlier established Yellowstone National Park with all its wonders awaiting me. I was in Yellowstone-Teton country, where I would quench my thirst in the fast, clear-flowing Snake River; where at Fishing Bridge I would throw my elk-hide mattress onto four inches of lodgepole pine needles. Here, for the first time, I would see rising trout roil the water like a rainstorm—20-inch native cutthroats feeding on caddis flies in the Yellowstone River.

I was hooked, first as a wildlife photographer and adventurer, later as a research ecologist and a log-home resident of the country often referred to as the Greater Yellowstone Ecosystem. It is a unit that includes all the physical, chemical, and biological elements necessary for the existence and perpetuation of a complex of animal and plant species. A tagged elk from the National Elk Refuge in Jackson Hole has traveled 95 miles north to the Lamar Valley in Yellowstone, giving an indication of the size of the ecosystem. Radio signals from collared grizzly bears have disclosed that some bears utilize home ranges embracing hundreds of square miles. Pronghorns summering on Antelope Flats within Grand Teton National Park stretch the ecosystem to the east and south when their late-fall migration returns them to the relatively snow-free desert near the upper Green River.

This Yellowstone country is a living entity composed of a variety of animals—pikas in specialized talus habitats; fluctuating populations of rodents; birds that arrive in spring, nest in summer, and are gone by winter; year-round residents such as ravens, ruffed grouse, goldeneye ducks and mergansers sharing open water and food with fish-eating otters. These and other species form animal communities interrelated and interdependent, requiring a healthy and diverse plant environment whose components are dormant in winter, growing and changing in spring and summer. These plants over time are replaced by others in an orderly succession, as from aspen and lodgepole to spruce and fir, a succession often initiated by fire and temporarily terminated by fire.

The vegetation of the Yellowstone ecosystem was, in places, drastically altered by the summer fires of 1988, but the ecosystem components remain and interrelated processes continue. The text and most of the photographs in this book predate the fire. Much of the ecosystem is depicted as it was, inviting comparisons of the past with the present and the future. This dynamic, still intact entity is Yellowstone country. Change is its most permanent characteristic; good management will ensure that irreversible changes do not occur.

Against a backdrop of charred lodgepole pine, an elk in Yellowstone feeds on grass that escaped the fires of 1988. Wildfires eventually burned over 1.4 million acres of Yellowstone country and affected about half of the park's 2.2 million acres. The blaze, one of the largest in U.S. history, involved 25,000 firefighters. Regeneration over eight years has restored grasses and other vegetation to soften the stark silhouettes of blackened snags.

YELLOWSTONE

COUNTRY

A Prologue

Yellowstone. The geysers spout. The mud pots burble. The hot springs simmer. The river roars through the canyon of yellow stone (that is also red and brown and white). At times the land quakes and, ever so slightly, rises and falls. "There is something very hot and very shallow under there," says a scientist who has measured the movements with laser beams and satellite signals. What is it under there? Semimolten rock, some speculate, perhaps three to five miles below the ground. Hot and shallow.

When the land moves up or down, Yellowstone Lake—about 136 square miles, with depths to 365 feet—shifts like water in a tilted basin. In the dead of winter, when the lake surface is an ice cake two feet thick, there are spots on the bottom near boiling. Bubbles percolate up from fissures; through a video camera the water looks like champagne.

Three times in the past two million years immense volcanic eruptions spewed hot ash and gas into the heavens and across the land. Fragments landed as far away as present-day California and Texas. The most recent eruptions began about 1.2 million years ago; lava flowed through cracks in the ground off and on for 600,000 years. Then came the blast, leaving a caldera in the form of a rough oval, some 30 by 45 miles, at the heart of Yellowstone country. Lava ran until 70,000 years ago. In 1980 Mount St. Helens flung out one ten-thousandth of the volume ejected at Yellowstone.

Over much of the high, cold country surrounding the Yellowstone caldera, volcanism spread thick layers of welded rhyolite ash; time has worn away hundreds of feet of it and topped what remains with a thin patina of soil. In that unpromising mix rose vast evergreen forests, mostly lodgepole pine. Fire and fierce winds and beetle infestations attack the forests: a spot here, a patch there—or, as in the historic summer of 1988, in leaping conflagrations that scorch hundreds of thousands of acres. Thus nature rearranges the woodland mosaic. Where trees die, light spreads across the forest floor. Grasses and other herbage grow in the openings, as they do along the margins of streams and in meadows enriched by glacial sediments. And the bighorns and the pronghorns in their hundreds, the bison and the deer in their thousands, and the elk in their tens of thousands harvest the green growth, high and low, as the seasons turn.

The gray wolf once again harvests the elk and the deer in this rich hunting ground, for the urge to restore nature's rhythms runs strong. The grizzly bear still harvests the elk and the bison—living and dead—and green growth, and fish that swim in the streams, and roots and nuts and berries and insects besides.

This is the great Yellowstone wonderland, our oldest national park and the largest outside of Alaska. Its wonders, of course, but also its harshness abetted the nation's resolve to preserve it. In 1872, the year of the park's birth, a congressional debater described it as "a region of country seven thousand feet above the level of the sea, where there is frost every month of the year, and where nobody can dwell upon it for the purpose of agriculture, containing . . . the most wonderful geysers ever found in the country."

So out of the Rocky Mountain wilderness emerged the world's first national park, a rectangular swath mostly in the northwest corner of Wyoming Territory, edging over into Montana and Idaho Territories. The park came into being before these territories became states. Almost from the time the park was born men sensed the existence of a greater Yellowstone, an interdependent web of mountain and meadow and forest and stream where wildlife roamed unbound by lines on maps. "If it were extended, so as to include winter and summer range," wrote Lt. Daniel C. Kingman of the park in 1886, "it might also afford a last resort and permanent abiding place for the large game of the country." Ironically, this farsighted concern for wildlife came from an Army engineer whose mission was to plan roads.

It was Kingman who conceived Yellowstone's Grand Loop, to allow "tourists to visit the principal points of interest without retracing their steps." The familiar figure eight does just that, though now it has become summer range for mechanized mastodons. When drivers halt to gaze at bison, vehicles choke the loop with the immovable and the irresistible. Around the time Kingman wrote, Gen. Philip Sheridan, noting the slaughter of Yellowstone elk for their hides, called for a park double the size of today's 2.2 million acres.

Such expansion never came, but Yellowstone was gloriously buffered. Nature had ringed it with mountain ranges—more than 40 peaks in the region top 10,000 feet. Some of the most awesome rise just to the south, in Grand Teton National Park. Our first national forest reserve, the Yellowstone Timberland Reserve, was set aside east of Yellowstone in 1891. Today, like the mountain ranges, national forests ring the park. One of them, the jointly administered Bridger-Teton, is the largest south of Alaska. Area wildlife refuges see to the care of elk, to the breeding of trumpeter swans, and to the surrogate parenting of whooping cranes.

There are mills with capacious appetites depending on the national forests for logs—and loggers depending on those forests for jobs. There are oil and gas underground and pumping and drilling rigs above. There's heat energy just beyond Yellowstone Park boundaries. How is it linked to the Yellowstone geysers? If it is tapped, what would happen to them, more than two-thirds of all the active geysers in the world? Nobody knows, but scientists' warnings are dire.

There's not much demand for "soft gold"—the beaver pelts that lured Jim Bridger, Jedediah Smith, trapper-diarist Osborne Russell, and the other mountain men into Yellowstone country. But there's hard gold in the mountains, and platinum and palladium and talc and travertine. And in lowlands where animals once found winter food and shelter, humans dwell. Yellowstone country encompasses all these, geysers and grizzlies, fire and frost, mountains and mines, human pursuits inside the preserves—and far beyond them.

*S*pring snow lingers on 12,000-foot peaks of Wyoming's Wind River Range

as outfitter Jim Allen leads a pack trip to the crest of the Continental Divide.

Glassy waters mirror a summer sunset on Shoshone Lake. Seekers of solitude,

like this canoeist, can escape year-round in Yellowstone's 2.2 million acres of wilderness.

*W*eather-beaten western faces of Grand, Middle, and South Teton reward

hikers in Grand Teton National Park; a lake nudges the foot of Schoolroom Glacier.

*W*inter oasis: Hot-water runoff from the Boiling River cascades into a

dammed pool in the Gardner River, warming two teenagers in January.

THE GRAND

MOSAIC

Spring Into Summer

*Nature prevails in the
Greater Yellowstone
Ecosystem, some 14
million acres of hot springs
and mountains, fields
and forests astride the
Continental Divide in
the northern Rocky
Mountains. A score of
man-made boundaries
slice through Yellowstone
country: two national
parks, all or part of seven
national forests, three
wildlife refuges, and an
Indian reservation. The
Green, the Snake, and
the Yellowstone Rivers rise
in the mountain fastness.*

*FOLLOWING PAGES: The
moon bows to the sun as
first light strikes the high
ridge of the Teton Range. In
the valley below, the Snake
River curls through wooded
flats. The mountains were
thrust up along a fault in
the earth's crust about nine
million years ago; the valley
sloped toward the peaks.*

O n a hazy, damp June morning a south wind snapped up the valley of Jackson Hole, Wyoming, as Michael Stewartt taxied his Cessna very gingerly. There were sage grouse strolling on the runway, and they took their sweet time yielding ground to the big bird. Well, they are kin to the spruce grouse, known far and wide as the fool hen. But something beyond foolhardiness drives these birds.

"It's their strutting ground," said Tim Clark, an ecologist from the town of Jackson, eight miles south of the airport. "The runway?" I ask. "Are you kidding?" No. Before there was a runway on this vast sagebrush flat, sage grouse had established a lek, where the cocks gathered to display and contend for hens. They still do, come pavement or Cessna or whining jetliner. The runway site boasts another distinction: We were in Grand Teton, taking off from the nation's only commercial airport in a national park. Conservationists fought the airport bitterly, but it happened. Like many others who resent the scarring of a great national park, I did not hesitate to use it. It was handy. In the mountains, claimed Old Gabe—Jim Bridger—nothing corrupts. I wondered.

On this late spring day my colleague, photographer Raymond Gehman, Dr. Clark, and I were off on a grand aerial loop to see how the parks and forests and refuges knit together in the Greater Yellowstone _____. People fill in the blank in a variety of ways. Clark and the scientific and conservation community would unhesitatingly say "Ecosystem," asserting the existence of a distinctive biogeographical tract of mountains surrounding the plateau that defines Yellowstone Park. It is one of the most intact ecosystems in the lower 48; most of the animal species nature put there are still there, even if, in a few instances, only in remnant populations.

Some people find "Ecosystem" impolitic, preferring "Area" or "Region" instead. The ecosystem concept implies coordinated management, resistance to widespread logging and development where they threaten the integrity of wildlife habitat or other resources. This conjures fears of more federal muscle in the heartland of the so-called Sagebrush Rebellion, fears expressed succinctly in the reaction attributed to one local citizen: "We don't need no ecosystem around here."

There are no legal boundaries for the ecosystem, and biology doesn't help much either in establishing firm lines. An ecosystem is a unit made up of living things and their nonliving surroundings and the interactions of those components. You can posit an ecosystem in a rotting log, a swamp, a valley—Tim Clark published a study of the Jackson Hole ecosystem. You can center it on a population of a single species, as pioneering researchers John and Frank C. Craighead, Jr., did in the 1970s when they referred to Yellowstone's grizzly bear ecosystem. You can employ a more inclusive approach—such as the Greater Yellowstone Ecosystem, a designation now more than a decade old.

Notions of the ecosystem's size range from 6 to 18 million acres. One version that has gained considerable currency

GREATER YELLOWSTONE ECOSYSTEM

Missouri R.

DEERLODGE N.F.

Bozeman

Livingston

Boulder

Stillwater

Yellowstone

Billings

BEAVERHEAD

Ennis

Virginia City

LEE

Spanish Peaks

METCALF

NATIONAL

WILDERNESS

Gravelly Range

FOREST

RED ROCK LAKES NAT. WILDLIFE REFUGE

MONTANA
IDAHO
Centennial Mountains

Henrys Lake

Island Park

TARGHEE

Big Springs

GALLATIN NATIONAL FOREST

Jardine
Gardiner

Mammoth

Hebgen Lake

Targhee Pass

West Yellowstone

Old Faithful

Shoshone Lake

Madison R.

YELLOWSTONE

Norris

Gibbon

NATIONAL

Firehole R.

PARK

Continental Divide

Bechler

Falls

ABSAROKA-BEARTOOTH

CUSTER N.F.

Beartooth Mts.

WILDERNESS

Cooke City

Red Lodge

Clarks Fork

Beartooth Plateau

BEARTOOTH HIGHWAY

MONTANA
WYOMING

NORTH

SHOSHONE

ABSAROKA

Canyon Village

Fishing Bridge

WILDERNESS

Yellowstone Lake

Lamar

Shoshone

Cody

North Fork

Thorofare Creek

NATIONAL

WASHAKIE WILDERNESS

Greybull

Wood

WINEGAR HOLE WILDERNESS

Henrys Fork

Teton

Teton Basin

NATIONAL

JEDEDIAH SMITH WILDERNESS

Falls

Snake

JOHN D. ROCKEFELLER, JR., MEM. PKWY.

Jackson Lake

Teton Range

GRAND TETON N.P.

Jackson Hole

TETON WILDERNESS

Two Ocean Pass

TETON

Moran

Togwotee Pass

NATIONAL

FOREST

WIND RIVER RANGE

Dubois

Owl Creek Mountains

Idaho Falls

Snake

Palisades Reservoir

Caribou Range

FOREST

Jackson Hole Ski Resort

Moose

NAT. ELK REFUGE

Jackson

FOREST

GROS VENTRE WILDERNESS

Gros Ventre Range

Hoback

BRIDGER

Union Pass

Whiskey Basin

Wind

FITZPATRICK WILDERNESS

Wind River

Indian

Reservation

GRAYS LAKE NAT. WILDLIFE REFUGE

CARIBOU

Freedom

NATIONAL

Salt River

Salt River Ra.

BRIDGER

WYOMING RANGE

NATIONAL

Snake River Range

NATIONAL

Green

Fremont Lake

Pinedale

FOREST

BRIDGER WILDERNESS

Cirque of the Towers

North Popo Agie

Lander

POPO AGIE WILDERNESS

SHOSHONE N.F.

Continental Divide

Great Divide Basin

Riley Ridge

FOREST

Montpelier

Bear

Wasatch Range

Bear Lake

IDAHO
WYOMING

40 km

40 mi

LANDS WITHIN THE ECOSYSTEM

National park land

National forest

Wilderness area within national forest

National wildlife refuge

Indian reservation

totals some 14 million acres—more than six times the size of Yellowstone Park—and measures as much as 250 miles north and south, and 150 east and west. In shape the map of this area reminds me of a headless colossus, teetering on crumbling legs. Its outline resembles those of the green areas in the road maps of Yellowstone country—the areas delineating the parks and forests.

A comprehensive government study entitled The *Greater Yellowstone Area, An Aggregation of National Park and National Forest Management Plans* used somewhat different boundaries; but an official who supervised the study had no real objection to the 14-million-acre version. The latter map, produced by the Wilderness Society, has been used by a team of researchers for a congressional committee and by the Greater Yellowstone Coalition, a high-profile, high-energy group of advocates for the preservation of the ecosystem.

In addition to the two parks, their map includes nearly ten million acres of national forests, some two-fifths of them designated as wilderness. All or parts of seven national forests—the Targhee, Beaverhead, Gallatin, Custer, Shoshone, Bridger-Teton, and Caribou—and three wildlife refuges, as well as some Bureau of Land Management and state and private land, form part of this mosaic. It was the first ecosystem map I encountered, and it proved to be a dependable guide for the rounds of Yellowstone country.

Michael Stewartt, at the controls of the Cessna, knew

Sure as spring, elk calves frolic around a young cow along the Madison River. A calf's white spots (above) help hide it from predators in the tall meadow grasses. Some dozen elk herds, totaling more than 90,000 animals, inhabit Yellowstone country. Other free-ranging animals that have roamed portions of the area since the Ice Age include the grizzly bear, the bighorn sheep, and the bison. Local ranchers denounced proposals to reintroduce the gray wolf.

the terrain well—both topographical and political. If you are of a certain age and grew up on Tom Swift novels, you would recognize Michael. He patrolled the Rockies, commanding an environmental air force. Chartered as the nonprofit Project Lighthawk, he and his team haul newspeople and potential allies over threatened wildlands and ravaged forests and polluting smelters, as low and as slow as the law and his aircraft permit. The close encounters win loyalty to the environmental cause, said Michael. Seeing is believing.

"Nature abhors an elevation," wrote Wallace Stegner, "as much as it abhors a vacuum; a hill is no sooner elevated than the forces of erosion begin tearing it down." The good news, for those of us who do not share the abhorrence, is that nature takes its time. So there on our left, as Michael steered north up Jackson Hole toward the plateau of Yellowstone, loomed the Tetons, like a wall of thunderheads, a line squall of rock, defining the beauty of mountains.

It seems impossible to imagine them much more imposing or magnificent. Yet they were. Today, the range rises more than 7,000 feet from Jackson Hole to the 13,770-foot summit of Grand Teton—a hypnotic surge, no piedmont, straight from flat to mountain mass. Some nine million years ago, when the Tetons pushed up and the valley dropped "like a giant trapdoor,"—in the words of Wyoming geologist David Love—the vertical offset, peak to floor, spanned 30,000 feet.

Southeast of the airport stretches the National Elk

"shapely wild animals in graceful silhouette, with twinkling feet"

–Olaus Murie
Wapiti Wilderness, 1966

Refuge, but the 8,000 or more winter refugees—except for a hundred or so yearlings—are gone to calving grounds and summer range, northwest into Grand Teton National Park, north as much as 65 miles to southern Yellowstone, north and east into the Bridger-Teton Forest. The bulls have left their antlers, dropping them in March and April and May and beginning to grow new ones before leaving for the highlands.

The old antlers are gone too. Jackson Cub and Boy Scouts have gathered them up, for sale to people who shape them into buttons and buckles and bolos, and to others who grind them into Oriental love potions. Part of the proceeds returns to buy alfalfa pellets. Through winter months when the snows are too deep or too crusty for the elk to reach the grasses, the refuge spreads the pellets, seven or eight pounds per elk, about half a dollar's worth each day—paid for partly by Wyoming hunting license fees, partly by the refuge, and partly, with the Scouts' help, by the elk themselves.

Elk once had much more room to roam through Jackson Hole for winter forage, but ranchers and settlements beginning in the late 19th century spread over a good part of the range. Elk starved in sickening numbers—it was said that you could walk for miles on the strewn carcasses. Concern over the elk situation brought the refuge into being in 1912.

Another great dying time, in 1927, brought to the valley Olaus Murie, who looked at wildlife with the eye of a biologist, artist, and writer. He discovered that many elk were dying in winter not of starvation but of a bacterial infection. Olaus recalled his "joy at the spring release of the survivors out onto the greening hillsides, up through the aspen groves, and on north to first verdure and new smooth red-brown coats and the endless freedom of the summer world."

With Olaus came the gifted Margaret, wife and chronicler of their scientific and wilderness adventures. "People with knowledge, and a majestic presence," says their old friend and colleague Dave Love. Olaus is gone, but Margaret has remained, gaining in majesty across the decades. I have heard her called the soul of the ecosystem. Her log house in Jackson Hole, where schoolchildren and conservationists and esteemed writers and scientists have come to pay their respects, concentrates the mind on the things that count—from the archive of research to the chipmunks that filch teatime cookies on the porch to a riveting view of the Grand Teton. I have edited a bit of her writing, a delightful chore, sought out the log house a few times, and, without formal invitation, silently took vows in the Mardy Murie cult of Jackson Hole.

Michael Stewartt steered northwest, skirting the John D. Rockefeller, Jr., Memorial Parkway—a road and a fillet of national parkland linking Grand Teton and Yellowstone—and crosses to the west side of the Teton Range. We were over the Jedediah Smith Wilderness of the Targhee National Forest. To the southwest spread the rolling grainfields of Teton Basin, surrounding Idaho towns settled by Mormon farmers.

From the basin the Tetons rise more gently, and from there one can see clearly the outlines of what French fur traders called *Les Trois Tétons,* the three teats. English speakers knew them for a time as the Three Paps and the Pilot Knobs. Today we know them as Grand, Middle, and South Teton. From the east, or Jackson Hole side, where most visitors encounter them, it is possible to pick out the three Teton peaks, enchanting, to be sure, but they do not look especially like tetons. There the old Indian names seem more apt: Hoary-headed Fathers, and Teewinot—Many Pinnacles.

Down in Teton Basin the fur brigades had a storied trading and carousing ground, the rendezvous site known as Pierre's Hole. In 1832 the men in the beaver trade—Tom Fitzpatrick, Joe Meek, the Sublette brothers among them—and Flathead and Nez Perce Indians had a wild rendezvous. Meek called it a "crazy drunk." Then came a band of Gros Ventre, allies of the feared Blackfeet. Shooting started, as many as 40 died, and the Battle of Pierre's Hole went down as the bloodiest encounter ever between Indians and mountain men.

Teton Basin plays host to a splendid rendezvous in modern days. Each September about 17,000 greater sandhill cranes wing into the valley; no other fall staging area in the Rockies counts so many. For a few weeks the big brown birds work the brown grainfields, then head south.

Near the high Targhee Forest passes Michael has just crossed, domestic sheep have grazed for years. It is also prime grizzly country. The mix was deadly, both for the sheep eaten by grizzlies and for the grizzlies shot by shepherds. Today, as a threatened species protected under the Endangered Species Act, the grizzly has priority here; when the bear starts marauding, the sheep must move.

We skirted the southwestern tip of Yellowstone Park, where the Bechler Canyon cleaves the Madison and Pitchstone Plateaus. This is known as Yellowstone's Cascade Corner for its fine waterfalls, and it ranks as some of the choicest backcountry in the park. A month before our flight a small earthquake occurred, centered on the Pitchstone; at Old Faithful, 15 miles away, the interval between eruptions changed as it does from time to time.

Flying north, we parallelled the park's western edge. We looked eastward into the low sun, across the golden expanse of Yellowstone Lake some 25 miles away. Midway between us and the lake steam rose from the thermals along the Firehole River, and among them a tall plume of water shot up. Old Faithful? Too far away to be certain.

Road maps of the boundary strip beneath us often look like a botched printing job, the colors out of register. That's because the park and the Wyoming-Idaho borders are about two miles apart, running parallel. From the air there's no mistaking the boundary here. Targhee and Gallatin National Forests have allowed loggers to cut to the very edge of the park. On one side a lodgepole forest; on the other, clearcuts. "Symbolically," said Tim Clark, "it's very dramatic, the

A wider world awaits a two-month-old red fox pup as it sniffs the air

outside its den in Red Rock Lakes Refuge. By late fall, the kit will set out on its own.

degree of human manipulation on both sides, the contrast of the two areas. Biologically, logging fragments the landscape in such a way that it breaks up animal populations and makes them more vulnerable to local catastrophes." Nearly three decades ago a massive infestation of mountain pine beetles in the lodgepoles led to a salvage timber sale program that made the Targhee the most heavily logged national forest, by far, in Yellowstone country.

Westward spreads a sprinkling of communities developed in Island Park, the 14-by-18-mile basin that formed during the Yellowstone volcanism. Experts speculate that there are reservoirs of thermal energy in it, under Targhee Forest jurisdiction and usable for heating and for spas. Yellowstone Park officials and environmentalists breathed a long sigh of relief when the forest decided to keep the reservoirs closed to exploration and commercial exploitation.

Near Island Park some 130 million gallons of cool pure water, enough to supply the households of nearly a million people, pour out of Big Springs each day to nourish Henrys Fork of the Snake River, a standout fishing stream in outstanding fishing country. The springwaters seem placid enough, until someone throws a chunk of bread in. Then they explode: This is a spa for fat rainbow trout, six- and seven-pound beauties flailing for the tidbits, which come with no strings attached. Big Springs trout are for ogling only.

The Continental Divide courses northwest out of Yellowstone Park to form the Montana-Idaho boundary, crosses Targhee Pass, and hooks around Henrys Lake, where in the

"She's our conscience," says an admiring neighbor in Jackson Hole. "A quiet conscience." With good heart and good words writer Margaret Murie has fought for unspoiled lands—sharing a rich and honored career with her late husband, Olaus Murie. Another Jackson Hole luminary, Frank C. Craighead, Jr., (below) combined wildlife research and wildland adventure. In pioneering bioecology studies Frank and his twin, John, advanced the idea of the Yellowstone ecosystem.

1870s Gilman Sawtell, provisioner for Virginia City miners and tourist wagons bound for wonderland, hauled out 40,000 trout a year. Beyond the lake the divide runs along the crest of the Centennial Mountains, the only range in the northern Rockies besides the Owl Creek that runs east-west.

Pioneer stockmen, driving cattle in a valley just to the north, named the valley in 1876 in honor of the nation's centennial of independence. Warm spring waters and the valley's remoteness provided a safe year-round haven for some trumpeter swans that survived the slaughter and habitat loss in Canada and across the lower 48 in the 19th century. The Red Rock Lakes National Wildlife Refuge was established here to protect the survivors and increase their numbers.

Near the eastern end of the Centennials, the Cessna lurched violently upward. "We've got a wind out of the southwest boiling over these mountains," said Michael. It jacked us up 400 feet.

*I*n Montana the national forests that form part of the Yellowstone ecosystem are the Gallatin, edging the western and northern bounds of the park, and a part of the Beaverhead, off to the northwest, where the Missouri River divides into three forks. The Lewis and Clark expedition came upon them in July of 1805. "Both Cap C. and myself," wrote Meriwether Lewis in his journal, "corrisponded in opinion with rispect to the impropriety of calling either of these streams the Missouri." Accordingly, the explorers named one fork for "the author of our enterprize," President Thomas Jefferson, another for Secretary of the Treasury Albert Gallatin, and the middle fork for Secretary of State James Madison.

The Jefferson River, westernmost fork, courses beyond Yellowstone country. The other two rise in the park. The Gallatin carves a beautiful canyon as it leaves the northwest corner and streams north toward the Spanish Peaks and Bozeman. In 1995 more than three million people visited the waters that form the Madison—the Gibbon and Firehole Rivers. Of nine geyser basins in Yellowstone, six lie along these waters.

From the famous junction of its two feeders, the Madison flows west, out of the park, into Hebgen Lake, then into the Madison Canyon, where a swath of brown and largely barren mountainside marks the great slide triggered by the earthquake of August 17, 1959. At least 28 people in the canyon that night were entombed or died of injuries.

In Yellowstone, geysers by the hundred erupted after the earthquake. One of them, Clepsydra, spouted for years without rest. Sapphire Pool turned from blue to muddy and shot up some of the most gigantic geyser eruptions known in the park, and then subsided. Today it is sapphire once again—but no longer erupts. Sapphire, says Rick Hutchinson, the park's thermal specialist, "blew its guts out."

At the north end of Hebgen Lake, near the epicenter of the quake, a developer sought a national forest permit for a

year-round resort, Ski Yellowstone. Environmentalists protested against such a major development less than ten miles from the park, noting the potential loss of priority grizzly habitat. For the first time computer modeling was applied to assess the cumulative effects of existing and proposed human activities on the grizzlies' use of the area. The study foresaw a potential hazard; Gallatin National Forest requested that the developer redesign Ski Yellowstone as a winter-only resort.

We flew north and east, across the Madison and Gallatin Ranges, sharply angled peaks and high lakes, where multiple-use and wilderness advocates contend for the future of undeveloped chunks of Gallatin National Forest. Before long we saw the Yellowstone River slanting northwest out of the park; the direction is only a feint, for the river soon swings northeast on its long reach across the plains, finally paying tribute to the Missouri at the Montana–North Dakota line. Lewis and Clark encountered it there, and Clark later explored upstream, but got no closer than some 60 miles to today's park boundary. They had heard from Indians that the river "waters one of the fairest portions of this continent."

The first recorded indication that the land was not only fair but also wondrous came in two letters written in 1805 by Gen. James Wilkinson, governor of the Louisiana Territory. Wilkinson wrote the secretary of war detailing his plans to finance a trip up the "River Piere jaune, or yellow Stone . . . which my informants tell me is filled with wonders." With the second letter he sent a map traced on buffalo hide to President Jefferson. We know no more of his plan; but Jefferson hung the map on a wall at Monticello, near a painting of St. Peter. A visitor called it an "odd union," but perhaps it is not so farfetched.

Tall lodgepole teeters in the grip of the one-armed Bunyan that just snipped it in Gallatin National Forest. On a steep slope Clayton Sherard (below) cuts trees the old way—an average of 300 a day, for 40 cents a tree. Loggers, environmentalists, and forest managers often clash over the impact of timbering on the ecosystem.

FOLLOWING PAGES: Tundra bouquet crowns a two-mile height above Twin Lakes along the Beartooth Highway, a scenic stretch of U.S. 212 that wriggles up and down granite cliffs between Cooke City and Red Lodge northeast of Yellowstone.

Pierre, Peter—both derive from the Greek word for "rock." Peter, the Gospels tell us, was the "rock" upon which Christ would build his church.

The valley of the Yellowstone has provided a corridor to the park from its earliest years. The gateway road threads the valley to the park, then bears south to the hub of Mammoth Hot Springs. From the air we can see the steaming travertine terraces of "White Mountain"—as Mammoth once was called. Nearby stand period-piece houses, in orderly array on tree-lined streets, an officers' row dating from the years between 1886 and 1918, when the U.S. Army patrolled the park, before the birth of the National Park Service.

Along the river corridor elk travel in fall and spring, to and from the winter feeding grounds known as the northern range. Lying mostly within the park, it is an area steeped in controversy, with scientists and graduate students taking vital signs year in and year out. Are there too many elk wintering over? Have they overgrazed the range? Short, direct questions produce complex and conflicting responses.

Bison share the range, and as their numbers have increased in recent decades, some drift out of the park. Montana, fearing the spread of brucellosis from bison to livestock and fearing also the bulldozer tactics of bison when farm fences stand in their way, legislated in 1995 that errant bison outside of the park be captured and slaughtered by Department of Livestock agents and that private landowners may shoot animals suspected of being diseased. During the winter of 1995-1996, 433 bison were destroyed by Park Service rangers and Montana Department of Fish, Wildlife, and Parks personnel, who then had jurisdiction over animals straying out of the park. While following this interim plan, the Park Service continues to look for solutions to satisfy nervous ranchers and bison that recognize no jurisdictions or boundaries.

Along this northwestern edge of Yellowstone spreads the spacious domain of the Church Universal and Triumphant, led by Elizabeth Clare Prophet, Guru Ma to her followers, and her husband and "soul mate," Ed Francis. The church property consists of tracts totaling about 33,000 acres. Development plans for the tract adjacent to the park are widely opposed as a threat to park resources, and the church, known in local headlines by the acronym CUT, is seen as a potentially dominant political force in the area.

The church denies it is a power-hungry cult and insists its activities will harm none of its neighbors, including the park. Just as in Island Park, proposals to tap a thermal spring on church property here raised a storm of concern. In response, Congress drew up legislation to provide protection for geothermal features within the park and funded a two-year study. Studies of the Corwin Springs area upstream from Bear Creek Springs concluded in 1990 found that if develpoment did not exceed the natural flow, then there would likely be no impact on thermal features within the park.

Some years ago a newspaper published a list of people whose opposition the church hoped to turn away by the power

of ritual. In the environmentalist circles of Bozeman and Livingston there was great dismay—among those who'd gone unmentioned. "If you weren't on that list," an activist told me, "your social standing around here plummeted."

Eastward we traversed the Absaroka-Beartooth Wilderness, a rugged northern buffer of young volcanic and ancient granitic mountains—the Absarokas, remnants of volcanic debris that erupted 30 to 50 million years ago, and the taller Beartooths, with rocks more than two billion years old. The wilderness lies in Gallatin, Custer, and Shoshone National Forests. Gold fever lured prospectors into this fastness in the 1860s; evidence of their reactions to the country dots the maps. One creek was a "hell roarer," another only "a slough." Hellroaring and Slough Creeks spill down into the park, the latter broadening into a handsome stream favored by seasoned Yellowstone flycasters. Between the two creeks prospector A. Bart Henderson in 1870 came onto a "beautiful flat" teeming with buffalo, elk, bear, deer, and moose—"the finest range in the world." He named it for the most numerous of the animals—the buffalo.

On a June day a century later we looked down on the fine range of Buffalo Plateau, meadows flushed with a welcoming green, specked with bison and—lighter in hue and in bulk—elk. The migrants had reclaimed their summer range. Michael descended a bit and throttled back—this scene was worth a slow pass or two. Bart Henderson might wonder at the bison numbers, far fewer now, but he would know this beautiful flat. Michael remembered flying the respected wolf researcher Dave Mech over Yellowstone's northern precincts. "He called it magnificent," noted the pilot. With all that prey, how could it be otherwise? Wolf country is wherever the moose and the elk and the deer are.

Weeks before, at a symposium in Washington, D.C., I had heard pleas for reasoned discourse on wolf restoration in Yellowstone. There were voices of doubt from ranchers who envisioned wolves rampaging out of the park into their herds. "You're coming in from Park Avenue," Montana stockman Joe Helle told his eastern audience, "and you want to put wolves in our backyard." There were voices of reassurance, from scientists such as Mech. And there were voices of hope. "Wolves can only enhance the impression of Yellowstone as primeval, pure, and whole," said Thomas McNamee, author of a detailed, at times lyrical, study of the grizzly bear. "You'll be able to see them stalking in Lamar Valley, see them sleeping on the ice. Human hearts will race with joy."

The prospectors of a century ago struck gold; at the site where Henderson found "gold in every gulch and sag," Cooke City arose. For decades local mines hauled ore and supplies through the park. Part of the legacy of those days lives on in denuded slopes and sterile sections of streams poisoned by acid drainage and heavy metals from the mines. Water quality continues to be a concern, and a legacy of mining, especially from tailings on creeks whose waters drain into Clarks Fork and ultimately into Yellowstone, is to create what some experts call a "biological desert." Delegates representing the World Heritage Committee visited Yellowstone in 1994 to determine if mining and other developments would jeopardize Yellowstone's status, and in August 1995 President Bill Clinton, on vacation in the Tetons, helicoptered over the site of a proposed mine and issued a two-year moratorium on claims, temporarily halting additional development.

Cooke City lives on today as a northeast gateway to Yellowstone and the western terminus of one of America's premier scenic roads, the Beartooth Highway. North of Cooke City we worked our way toward the hard steep face of Granite Peak, highest point in Montana at 12,799 feet. A long ridge, freshly powdered with snow, arcs southward from the peak. Beyond the ridge rises Tempest Mountain, at the head of Froze to Death Plateau. Cold, tempestuous country, the Beartooth, spiked with 12,000-footers.

On the northern face of the mountains, near the Absaroka-Beartooth Wilderness, miners each day blast hundreds of tons of ore containing metal more precious than gold. The mine on the Stillwater River is unique—the only significant source of platinum and palladium in the nation.

When work began on the Beartooth Highway in the early 1930s, Ernest Hemingway glumly envisioned it as the ruin of a happy hunting ground. The Cessna took us southward over that ground now, the mountain-girt Wyoming valley of the Clarks Fork of the Yellowstone. The stream marks the approximate junction between the Absarokas and the Beartooths as it foams through a dark, plunging canyon. It is a wild and scenic river, de facto; local citizens wanted it protected as such, a Wild and Scenic River, de jure, and a 21-mile stretch was so designated in 1991.

Hemingway thought the highway would drive the game into the sanctuary of Yellowstone just to the west. He loved to come here, to a dude ranch, indulging what one literary critic has called his "devotion to blood sports." He learned the ways of the trout, of the bighorn sheep, and of the grizzly. This was decades before the Endangered Species Act, and Hemingway took fondly to the local pastime of killing a mule as bait for grizzlies, then dropping the bears that took the bait. Biographer Carlos Baker paints a memorable picture of the novelist eating grizzly steak, medium rare, sandwiched between sourdough pancakes, the famous beard streaked with bear grease.

We passed on south to the country of Buffalo Bill Cody, where a busy road runs from Cody, the town he helped found in 1896, west along the campgrounds and dude ranches of the Shoshone National Forest to the east entrance of the park. Here too runs a famous stream, known through the 19th century as the Stinking Water River, for a sulfur spring near Cody; it is known today as the North Fork of the Shoshone River. John Colter, the mountain man, encountered it in the winter of 1807-08, as he did the Clarks Fork. He may also have been the first

FOLLOWING PAGES: Hiker's daydream from a perch above the Yellowstone River Delta might include visions of fur trappers trekking into the uncharted wilds of Yellowstone country. Coming for beaver pelts in the early 19th century, these tough, buckskin-clad mountain men passed through this region—called the Thorofare—en route from the headwaters of the Yellowstone River to the valley of Jackson Hole. Awestruck mountain men first described Yellowstone's shooting geysers and steaming springs.

"paint cannot touch it and words are wasted"

-Frederic Remington
Pony Tracks, 1895

45

white man to see Jackson Hole and the wonders of Yellowstone; more than a century of debate hasn't settled the point.

Eventually the trappers established well-traveled routes into Yellowstone and Jackson Hole. One of them, beneath us now, in the Teton Wilderness of the Bridger-Teton National Forest, came to be known as the Thorofare. The route links the headwaters of the Yellowstone, south of the park, with Two Ocean Plateau and the Snake River drainage into Jackson Hole.

At Two Ocean Pass, wrote trapper Osborne Russell in an oft-quoted diary entry, the waters divide, one side "bound for the Pacific and the other for the Atlantic ocean. Here a trout of 12 inches in length may cross the mountains in safety." Indeed, that is how the cutthroat trout got into Yellowstone Lake and the upper river—by crossing the gentle divide from the Snake to the Yellowstone drainage.

Decades after Osborne's diary note, Nathaniel P. Langford, the first superintendent of Yellowstone, reported, "the park is only accessible from Montana. It is impossible to enter it from Wyoming." Those Wyoming mountains would make the park useless to the territory, it was said; Montanans sought to annex wonderland.

Indians and trappers had done the "impossible"; somehow the lore faded away. Beaver hats had gone out of style, and by 1840 most of the mountain men had gone out of the mountains. So in 1873, when the Shoshone Indian guide Togwotee led

Below ice-carved peaks of the Cirque of the Towers, in the Wind River Range, guide Jim Allen leads a pack string across the North Popo Agie River. Early sunlight silvers a fragrant stand of spruce and white pine (opposite) as Jim and his dog Rusty stroll near camp at Lizard Head Meadows. "I do it for love, not for money," says Jim of his job. "My clients can get a glimpse of days gone by and experience the world of the mountain men."

49

Light and shadow streak 11,884-foot Pingora Peak, in the Cirque of the

Towers. Lonesome Lake mirrors the granite crag, which lures climbers to the Wind Rivers.

Army Capt. William A. Jones to a crossing south of the Thorofare, the captain exulted in his conquest of an "impassable barrier never scaled by white man or Indians." He named it Togwotee Pass. Today it serves as a passageway to Jackson Hole from the east. The Absaroka Range rises to the north, the Wind River Range to the south.

We skirted the west face of the Winds. Near Union Pass, Michael Stewartt pointed to old clear-cut strips. "Pure boondoggle logging," he said. The cuts are decades old; here the forest returns slowly. Environmentalists liken such tracts to "moth-eaten carpets." Southward we passed over the Green River Lakes, headwaters of the third great river system of Yellowstone country—the Green River, bound for the Colorado and the Gulf of California. In late morning the wind pitched us about; thunderheads rose. The most violent storms in this region sweep up from the southwest. The Wind Rivers, first major range on the storm track, contain the most glaciated mountains in the ecosystem. Also the tallest peak—Gannett, at 13,804 feet. Also the most ancient rocks—zircon 3.8 billion years old, rock as old as any on the continent.

When the mountains formed, they folded over, exposing limestone, rich in calcium, on the east side, and granites that pushed out over and buried the limestone on the west. Elk and deer antlers grow bigger on the eastern slopes. Pinedale, on the west side, draws its drinking water from glacial Fremont Lake, one of the purest lakes in the nation. "You can put that water in your battery," says one resident. But the pure water from high, granitic lakes has its drawbacks. Calcium-poor, it doesn't do much for development of strong teeth. "I could always tell Pinedale kids when they smiled," says David Love. This southeastern mountain corner of the ecosystem includes part of the Wind River Indian Reservation. Home of Shoshone and Arapaho, it spreads into the plains, over an area as large as Yellowstone Park.

Freedom from the law inspired the name of a one post-office town southwest of Grand Teton National Park. Mormon polygamists who founded the town a century ago chose a site straddling the Idaho-Wyoming border. Many sidestepped state laws and maintained a family in each jurisdiction. Main Street now bisects the town. All 550 residents must pick up their mail in Wyoming.

We turned west away from the Winds, toward the southwest leg of the ecosystem. Here the mountain ranges are little known under their own names—the Wyoming, Salt River, Snake River, and Caribou Ranges; but they are world famous as links in the Overthrust Belt of the Rockies, some rich in oil and gas.

Unlike the Winds and the Beartooths and other Yellowstone country mountain ranges rising from granite roots, says David Love, these are "rootless" mountains that "shimmied" across the land. They began as sheets of sedimentary rock, some as far as 75 miles to the west, and in the upheaval that produced the Rockies were thrust eastward like cards from a deck. The upper ones, subjected to the least friction, moved farthest. And here they rise, roughly parallel, trapping pools of treasure just east of the Idaho-Wyoming boundary. Producing wells near Riley Ridge, part of the Bridger-Teton Forest in the Wyoming Range, are tapping one of the largest gas-bearing structures in the contiguous states.

Westward, in the marshes of Grays Lake National Wildlife Refuge, surrounded by Caribou National Forest, biologist Rod Drewien spent a dozen springs and summers playing nursemaid to hatchling and juvenile whooping cranes. He wanted most of all to succeed as matchmaker, to establish a breeding population of this struggling species. At times a whooper or two flies up to Yellowstone Park, a welcome return to historic range.

We flew north with the long ridges of the rootless ranges. Near journey's end we passed over the Snake River Canyon, looking down on a river far more energetic than the tranquil Snake of Jackson Hole. Here it becomes *La Maudite Rivière Enragée*—The Accursed Mad River—of the French voyageurs. In summertime it becomes a frothy conveyor belt for waves of rafters and kayakers. At Jackson the rootless mountains butt up against the granite-cored, younger Gros Ventre Range to the east and the Tetons to the west. We dipped into the valley and touched down. I had, in a way, completed a grand round of Greater Yellowstone. In fact, it was only a skim. I had to get closer, to the Yellowstone witchery, to the Teton majesty, to the forests and the sanctuaries, to summer's freedom, autumn's turning, winter's hush.

*W*hite water boils
around river
runners in Snake
River Canyon in the
Targhee National Forest.
One of the 100,000
vacationers who challenge
the Snake each year, a
kayaker bounces through
a frothy rapid. Most boat
passengers manage to hang
on (above), though high
waves swallow a craft now
and then (above opposite).

FOLLOWING PAGES:
Beyond a stray horse, bands
of 55-million-year-old
sedimentary rocks ribbon
the Dubois Badlands. As
fragile as it is spectacular,
the Yellowstone ecosystem
developed over eons;
now human users must
cooperate to ensure its
existence through
coming centuries.

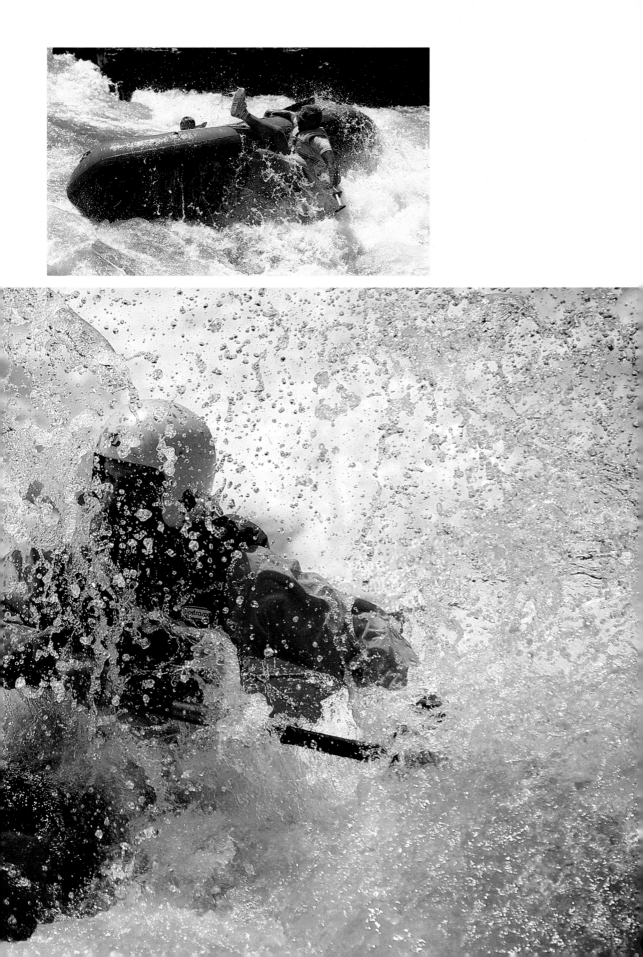

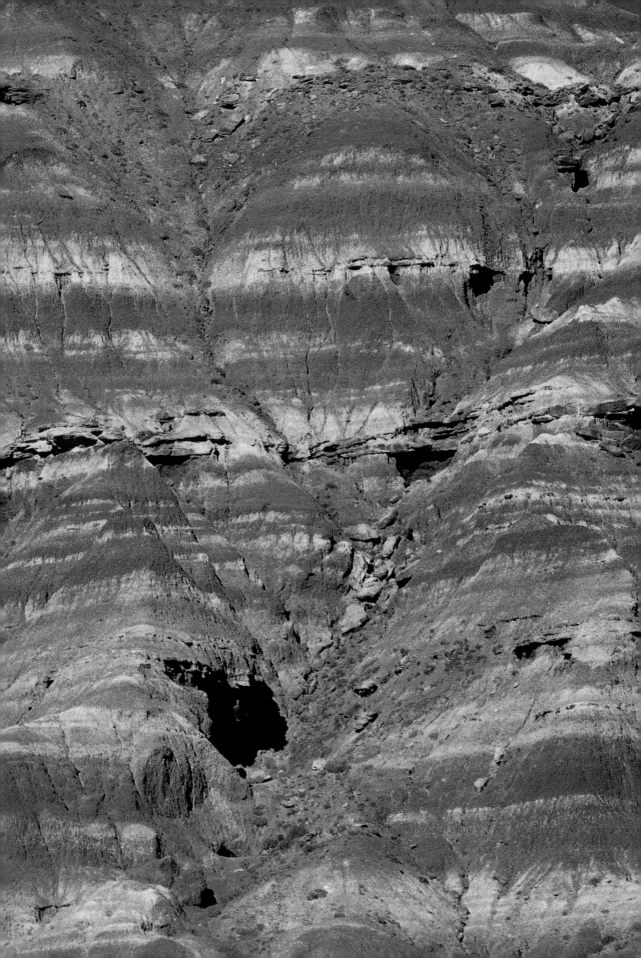

YELLOWSTONE

NATIONAL PARK

Summer

She was lively and, through the glasses at least, quite glamorous. The golden highlights of her coat rippled in the sun like ripe grain as she and her offspring meandered across the meadows. To thousands of visitors she brought hours of unexpected pleasure. Yet those who knew her best looked on with growing concern. They knew, as she didn't, that for a grizzly bear in Yellowstone, human beings are bad company. Grizzlies tend to steer clear of people places; this one sought them out. Like all of her kind here, she had no name. She did have a number: 104, the 104th bear fitted with a radio collar since 1975. She was a young mother, one of the youngest known in these parts, and people who studied her thought that might account for her lack of caution. No one really knew. So, while visitors surged to wherever she showed herself, rangers and biologists in and out of Yellowstone tracked her and moved her, and also tried to jolt her away from the roadsides with aversive conditioning. She made progress in this school of hard knocks, but it was not enough.

An ambient giddiness, swelled by the sight of a grizzly wild and free with scampering cubs, stirred subversive thoughts. I rooted for 104 against the omnipresent management crews and their traps and tranquilizers and hand-held radios. Go way. Let her be. But I had heard, again and again, the tales of bears addicted to human surroundings, the temptation of human foods. Such grizzlies quickly become a problem, then all too often a hazard, and, finally, a target. In the end I wished 104 would go away, deep into the wild heart of Yellowstone, that I would not hear of her again.

Whether a grizzly population of healthy size can maintain itself even there—that thicket of controversy fills volumes. Better to remain giddy for a while, around the meadows swelling into summer, the ancient forests turned to stone, the spawning streams teeming with cutthroat, the long cleft of canyon with its heat-tinted walls, the boiling geysers.

On a clear, brisk morning in June, Old Faithful did not draw a crowd. There was no room at the inn, of course; dark, dormered Old Faithful Inn fills up quickly. But few cars coursed the freeway-style approaches, the big loops of concrete that seem so misplaced here. They will find their uses in the midsummer crush, when Rudyard Kipling's anguished reaction to the multitudes echoes across the decades: "Today I am in the Yellowstone Park, and I wish I were dead."

This day was not that kind. Empty benches surrounded the low gray mound that brings forth the charming inn and the charmless roads, that brings the crowds and keeps the faith. A trio of women, visitors from the Orient, stood hunched and shivering. Herb Warren, retired a dozen years and summoned to a new calling, glanced at his watch and returned to a patient gaze at the steam venting up and streaming away from Old Faithful.

Now water joined the steam, jetting up 10, 20 feet, beginning a low roar, to my ears like water plunging into a tight

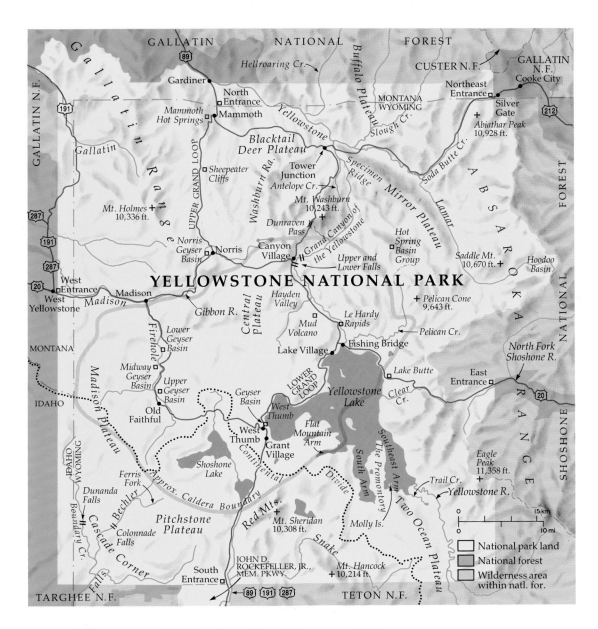

canyon. Warren recorded the time. The visitors watched perhaps a minute, then quickly departed, half running for the warmth of the inn a few hundred yards to the west.

"Wait," Warren called after them. "It's only preplay." No response. Warren shook his head. "It's a shame those folks left. I couldn't convey to them that there's a better show coming." And there it was. Preplay over, the shaft of boiling water rose, 50, 80, 120 feet—the naked eye could only guess. The eruption may leap as high as 180 feet. When the geyser had played out to the last gurgle of water and returned to a plume of steam, Herb Warren marked the time again. This was a short one, one minute, 58 seconds, and so he could predict that it would be only a short interval, 50 minutes or so, before Old Faithful filled its reservoir with groundwater, built a head of superheated steam under pressure, and blew off again.

At this early hour no ranger was on duty to do what Herb Warren had volunteered to do. In the lobby of the inn he

Heads Up! Something ahead startles Bear 104 and her cubs near the park's East Entrance. Atop Mount Washburn, whose slopes provide habitat for grizzlies and views for hikers, an Italian visitor wrote in the lookout log, "Bellissimo spettacolo. Ma dove sono gli orsi? Most beautiful spectacle. But where are the bears?" The answer: mostly in the wild. But in 1986 and '87 Bear 104 and her cubs took to foraging, frisking, and rubbernecking around Washburn and beyond the East Entrance. Bear management teams, fearing she would endanger herself as well as the delighted tourists, moved her to the wilds.

posted his prediction; I noted that he advanced the time by several minutes. "You cheat a little," he said with a spreading smile. "People tend to go out precisely. If the geyser goes off a few minutes early, then they miss it. This gives them a better chance." In days gone by a bellhop roused the guests, calling out the geysers that were "a-goin off!"

We were in the renowned, cavernous lobby of logs and limbs cut from the nearby forest, with the two tiers of balconies rising to a ceiling ridge 92 feet high, with the four-sided fireplace formed of 500 tons of rough-cut local stone—a fantasy of lodgepole Gothic crafted early in the century by the celebrated architect of Yellowstone, Robert C. Reamer. Earthquake and alteration over the years did not enhance Reamer's work, but a restoration in 1987-88 was partially guided by his vision. And why not? The vision produced what historian Charles Francis Adams called the one "man-made structure in the Park that looks as though it grew there."

The inn does not face the geyser that inspired it. Reamer aligned the building so that guests arriving at the porte cochere

would see Old Faithful directly ahead, to the east. Later, Reamer added two wings, and one of them does front the geyser. I spent a night in the east wing, in a plain room, sparsely furnished. In the morning sunlight flooded in; when Old Faithful turned up its nozzle, the sun inflamed the spouter, and the windows took that in too. Now the lackluster room glowed with the luster of a world-class view.

Herb Warren, a Coloradan in his 70s who ran bowling lanes and a restaurant before retiring, took an east-wing room for the summer. "I leave my window wide open, and quite often Old Faithful wakes me, and I time it and set my alarm for the next eruption," he said. Like a handful of other geyser-gazers enraptured by the mystery and beauty of the thermal fields, he was an official volunteer, his observations adding both to the store of data and to the public enjoyment.

Old Faithful does not go off like clockwork. It is simply the most faithful of the big geysers, not the biggest, not as powerful as some of its neighbors in the roughly two-square-mile Upper Geyser Basin ("upper" in the sense that it is the farthest upstream along the Firehole River, just a few miles below the Continental Divide). Grand is the tallest predictable geyser in the world, shooting up as high as 200 feet, but it rests for at least six hours, sometimes more than half a day between performances. Giant Geyser chuffs and puffs uproariously from a broken, 10-foot-high cone, and geyser-gazers await the day when it will redeem its reputation as one of the "mightiest geysers" in Yellowstone.

Hot geyser water dissolves silica from the subterranean rocks and deposits it at the surface as sinter as the water cools, runs off, and evaporates. The sinter, or geyserite, may form a mound, as at Faithful, or a cone, as at Giant. Fountain geysers, such as Grand, have no cone; they erupt from a pool or simply a funnel-shaped hollow in the ground. And some cone geysers do not look at all like cones. Castle looks like the hulk of a castle, or, in my fancy, the superstructure of a submarine, hull submerged. At Grotto, sinter sheaths dead logs, creating the most fanciful shape, a pillar and curls and hollows—the rhythms of Henry Moore's abstract sculpture.

With luck, a willingness to wander the basin, and a strategy refined by the Old Faithful naturalists, it is possible to enjoy a feast of geysers in a morning. Faithful, for sure; Grand, pumping up in spurts; Castle, splashing, then spouting steam for an hour or so; Daisy, star of its own group just west of the Firehole; and Riverside, one of the prettiest of all, with a grassy rise behind it, the geyser not shooting straight up but hosing out across the river.

There by the side of the Firehole, against a lodgepole, notepad and pen in hand, crouched John Wegel one day. Wegel, it seems fair to say, could not take his eyes off Riverside—not merely the graceful arc dimpling the stream, but also the lengthy preplay, one to two hours long. Every little surge and splash

The Yellowstone country grizzly, tracked and studied by researchers, takes priority over much of its roughly six-million-acre key habitat (map, below). Officials have tentatively identified the yearling (opposite) as Bear 122, a female slain by a poacher in 1986. Man-caused deaths of adult females, scientists say, can seriously hinder the effort to maintain a stable grizzly population.

FOLLOWING PAGES: Winding toward the Washburn Range, the Yellowstone River cleaves Hayden Valley.

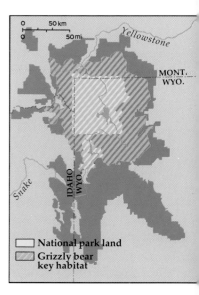

National park land
Grizzly bear key habitat

Reflections of a dying sun stain the Firehole River and steaming hot springs.

Mountain man Jim Bridger called Yellowstone "a place where hell bubbled up."

and dribble from the vents of the chair-shaped cone intrigued him. Wegel told me he had been watching Riverside since 1977. One summer he had recorded 500 consecutive eruptions—every single one for three months. When we met he was nearing 50 years of age, sleeping in his car and eating out of cans—he had no time for cooking. He had been trained as an engineer, but pursued his vocation only here. "My father left me some money," he explained. "I never really got started in life, so this is important to me, because it's a good research project, I can promise you that."

He had analyzed in massive detail the sequence of events that precede a Riverside eruption. He also determined that Riverside is bimodal. The time between eruptions is about 6 hours, 20 minutes or 7 hours, 15 minutes. There's no telling in advance which one it will be. But then John Wegel was not through studying Riverside.

Winter dies hard in Yellowstone, some years harder than others. That one did not linger. It would mean a smaller winterkill of elk and moose and deer, and slimmer pickings for the bears rousing from dens in March and April. Thawing carcasses provide a rich source of protein after the long fast. A mild winter would advance the salad days for grizzlies and black bears, with the early sprouting of spring beauty and juicy grasses. A light snowpack would mean a shorter runoff of melt-water, and the early arrival of the spawning cutthroat in the streams where the bears come to fish.

That year all the gates of Yellowstone opened by mid-April, some three weeks before they usually do. Although it had been a mild winter, there had been seven inches of ice to shave off some of the roads, ice packed by the winter traffic of thousands of snow machines. But that was done, and the big rotary plows headed up to Dunraven Pass, at 8,859 feet the highest point on the Grand Loop. It is just beyond Canyon Village and it was not yet basking time up there.

In May, Kevin Pierson, a bartender from the northern gateway town of Gardiner, Montana, came out to do a little fishing west of Canyon, at Wolf Lake. He lost his way, and the rangers went looking for him. He heard their loudspeaker; they didn't hear his yells. The night got frosty. He put his butane lighter to dead pine duff; too damp. His map, burning, provided small comfort. Then he turned to higher-priced fuel in his wallet. "I had five singles and some Belgian money I got out of a cereal box," Kevin recalled. "I burned a bunch of business cards too. But I saved the family pictures. I was in a swamp and I was desperate, and I kept hugging a tree, hoping Yogi wouldn't get me." The rangers found him soon after daybreak as he was walking out.

In early June of that precocious spring, visitors rolled into Canyon Village, a major park development with a shopping center, already open, and a campground and a sprawl of cabins, both still closed. There was pressure to open the campground early—before the scheduled date and before the summer rangers were due in. But an unexpected visitor checked into the campground area—Bear 104, with her cubs—and that mooted the issue for a few days.

Some of the best bear habitat in the park lies just an

Defying a summer drizzle, visitors stroll the boardwalk in the Upper Geyser Basin. Hundreds of geysers, along with other hydrothermal features, dot the Yellowstone region, where molten rock lies nearer the earth's surface than in most other places in the world. Diverse life-forms thrive in and add color to the hot springs. Silvery geyserite, a mineral deposited by thermal waters, surrounds a pool (below); bacteria that survive in temperatures as high as 162°F stain the water green and yellow.

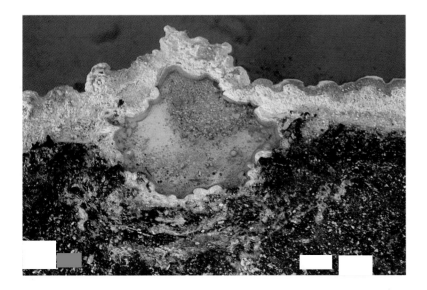

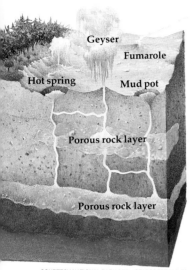

Geyser

Fumarole

Hot spring

Mud pot

Porous rock layer

Porous rock layer

COURTESY NATIONAL PARK SERVICE/ ROBERT HYNES

easy ramble away—in the Washburn Range to the north and in the valleys to the south and east. You cannot pitch a tent at Canyon. "Warning," read the sign at the campground entrance. "Hardsided Vehicles Only. Closed to tents, tent trailers, pop-up vans, and sleeping on the ground. Area frequented by bears."

June, advancing spring—and it was still not basking time here. One morning snow whipped around in stinging flurries. "Graupel snow," said Mark McCutcheon, head ranger at Canyon. Hard pellets, heralding a cold front. This was not bad news; cold might make an invigorating companion today. I had joined Mark on a spring-cleaning trip to backcountry campsites some five miles distant—the last two miles descending some 1,400 feet, all the way down a Grand Canyon wall to the Yellowstone River. Mark remembered an old description of the trail: "Five miles in and 35 miles out." A hot day would add miles.

Water of melting glaciers cut the Grand Canyon of the Yellowstone to its present shape, and heat from the great Yellowstone caldera colored it. Weighty evidence of the ice lies right at the trailhead—a 500-ton boulder of gneiss, measuring 24 by 20 by 18 feet, more than a billion years old. It sits on canyon rimrock that welled up out of the caldera less than a million years ago. The nearest gneiss outcrop lies 15 miles away. Glacial ice, which once covered most of Yellowstone to a depth of 3,000 feet, pushed the boulder to its resting place atop the young rock. Advancing glaciers choked the canyon, and the floods of melting glaciers recarved it, cutting through soft layers of rhyolite lava to form a gorge some 20 miles long, 1,500 to 4,000 feet wide, up to 1,500 feet deep. And hot steam and gas cooked the rhyolite walls to a vivid turn.

We walked the rim trail through biting squalls, in lodgepole forest patched with a ground cover of grouse whortleberry; we looked across sedge meadows to peaks of the Washburn Range and across the canyon to see Silver Cord Cascade cutting a fine line down the Yellowstone tuff, the welded ash of the canyon walls. Silver Cord drops about 1,000 feet, one of the longest cascades in Yellowstone. The trail switchbacked down through slopes of geyserite, amid steaming cones and vents, past swift and smelly Sulphur Creek, to where the glossy green river raced through the gorge. This was Seven Mile Hole, a flat spot in the canyon seven miles down the Yellowstone from Lower Falls. A year earlier a hiker had twisted an ankle down here. Mark thought of a helicopter, but when he stomped on the geyserite flats, he heard hollow rumblings. A surefooted horse, backed by a reserve of six rangers and a litter, hauled out the hiker. Mark and I hauled out slowly and wheezily, pausing eagerly to drink and snack, and to welcome the cooling gusts of snow.

Millions of visitors each year find easier routes to the Grand Canyon—roads on both rims leading to storied viewpoints, from Inspiration Point on the north side to Artist Point on the south. I joined the auto stream and paused at each viewpoint, a half day well spent. The changing panorama sweeps around a gaudy rock palette of red, brown, white, and orange. On a jut of rock high above the river lies a pile of brush; an osprey makes its home there. Just below Artist Point, steam rises from a tiny cone—the very model of a science-fair volcano.

At the head of the canyon, Upper Falls plunges 109 feet into a rocky amphitheater, with rainbows rising in the veil of spume. The river rushes on for a half mile, then bursts from narrowing walls, spewing broad white tresses down the 308 feet of Lower Falls. Uncle Tom's Trail leads toward the foot of Lower Falls. Originally the descent was by ladder. In 1889 someone sought to build an elevator, but the park superintendent of the day would not have it. Today hikers descend 328 metal steps—something like a 30-story fire escape. There is no escape from the climb back up.

"For a bear's-eye view of Yellowstone," read the entry in the schedule of ranger-led activities, "join Ranger Barb on a bear country hike." Can it be? I wondered, knowing what she's been through. Sure enough. Barbara Pettinga gathered us at the Fishing Bridge Visitor Center one cold, wet Monday morning and set out on a three-hour hike and a much longer span of memory. She is an artist and educator from Shelburne, Vermont, a grandmother and a summer naturalist. "I have had a close encounter of the grizzly kind, and if you like, I'll share it with you later," she said as we started out, about a dozen strong, from the Mud Volcano area at the southern edge of Hayden Valley. A few hikers already knew a bit of bear country lore; they came with bear bells. One brought a stick for banging against trees.

"The possibility is almost nil," said Barbara, "but if we should see one, don't anyone run. Let's stick together. When you're in a group the bear is less likely to attack." We walked in the open, well away from the forest edge. We wanted to be seen. Someone asked about the kinds of trees in the forest. "When I'm in bear country," Barbara joked, "I recognize only two kinds of trees—those that I can climb and those that I can't." The climbing kind does not guarantee safety; grizzlies usually won't climb trees, but they can.

We paused amid some hot springs around a heap of bison bones that a grizzly had crunched. "I'm going to tell you what happened to me," she began. "There are some strong safety messages in it. And there's also the realization that some situations are unavoidable. You've done nothing wrong. You just happen to be in the wrong place."

In the summer of 1984 she and her late husband, Bob, an aeronautical engineer, came through some trees toward a vantage for a spacious view of Hayden Valley. About 200 feet away she spotted a bison carcass. "I stepped out maybe five or six paces to look at it through my binoculars," she went on. "Bob stayed back in the trees. He felt uneasy. He looked out to the right just as the bear raised her head. She was bedded down in a little cluster of trees. Around 80 feet away. They measured it afterward." There were two cubs with the

Complex underground plumbing shapes the hydrothermal attractions of Yellowstone (opposite). The thinness of the earth's crust in the region, abundant precipitation, and the presence of underlying porous rocks all contribute. Surface water percolates through porous rock toward deep molten rock called magma. Superheated by a layer of hot rock above the magma, the water forces its way back to the surface. Water rising through a clear route emerges as a hot spring. A constricted channel that restricts the flow of very hot water may result in a spouting geyser. Where little moisture builds up, a fumarole vents steam. Bubbling mud pots result when acidic water and gases break rocks into fine clays and carry them to the surface.

FOLLOWING PAGES: Old Faithful joins Old Glory in a Fourth of July celebration at Yellowstone National Park.

sow, a bison carcass nearby, and a surprise intrusion—a recipe for trouble. "He yelled, `Barb, Barb, look out!' I turned around and in just that length of time the bear had rolled onto her feet and was in a charge.

"So what do you do?" Barbara broke the spell with a rhetorical question. Someone said he'd faint. A youngster said he would crouch down. "Yes. Some people recommend that you get into the cannonball position. . . . Do you want to demonstrate?" She got the boy rolled up, with his hands clasped over his neck, showing how the position protected face and soft parts. "Thank you very much, Christopher, that was a good cannonball."

She resumed. "No, I didn't get into a cannonball position. I stood facing the bear and I just started to back off. I was absolutely terrified. The last I remember was seeing that bear's head coming toward me." Bob Pettinga saw the grizzly grab his wife's thigh and flip her. She landed face down, backpack up— thus with a bit of protection. "Almost immediately I realized I had to play dead . . . not make any struggle or any noise at all. She left me, as soon as I did that. She left me and went after Bob."

He had had time to get into a cannonball crouch. The bear bit him above one knee, broke away, ran upslope, and came back down. "She ran right over his back," Barbara continued, "and came out at me again. She put her claws under my uphill side and pulled me over onto my back. There was a lot of momentum and I used it to get face down again. She did that three times. Then she left, she cleared out with the cubs and we never saw her again."

The grizzly left scars on her body, but none on her mind or spirit. Yellowstone remains a land of enchantment for her, the more so for the presence of grizzlies. She regards the one that attacked her as "a good bear. She did what she had to, protected her family and food, and left me without permanent damage." It was different with Bob Pettinga. "In some ways," Barbara told me, "the encounter was worse for him. This is kind of a paradox. My injuries were far more serious. Consequently I went through the buffering experience of being in shock." With Bob, she feels, "it was not so much what happened to him, but what happened to me and having to watch it helplessly. He was less than eager to do any major hiking in the park afterwards. I sometimes go to great lengths to get together a group for a backcountry outing, but I never hike alone."

Hayden Valley, rolling across the center of the park, throbs with life. Its silty soil, residue of an ancient lake bed, encourages sagebrush and grass rather than conifer forest. The Yellowstone River, flowing north from Yellowstone Lake to the Grand Canyon, cuts the wide valley in long, lazy arcs, with faint rifflings and stirrings on the deep green surface. Shoals of waterbirds frequent the stream, Canada geese, white pelicans, mallards, even some harlequin ducks.

Getting everyone in the picture—in the one and a half to five minutes that Old Faithful erupts—prompts a relay race by the Lai family of Elmhurst, Illinois. Joseph Lai snaps a picture; then mother, Vivian, grabs the camera to photograph Joseph and their children. Named for its dependable displays, Old Faithful has been a reliable performer throughout the park's history. Best known of Yellowstone's thermal features, it attracts up to 25,000 visitors each day.

*Seven stories tall, the lobby
of the Old Faithful Inn
bustles with activity in
summer. Like Michael and
Sara Leon (above), visitors
can always find a quiet
niche in the old hostelry.
Built of local timber and
stone, it has delighted
guests since it opened in
1904; 500 tons of volcanic
rock went into the
enormous fireplace. One
early client called the inn
"the most unique and
perfect place," his room,
"a paradise of restfulness
though in a rough and
rustic fashion."*

Elk and bison graze here, and from the road parallel-ing the river stop-and-start streams of summertime tourists watch the show. In early summer the elk look red and sleek. Often the bulls present their velvety antlers in profile, with a graceful twist of the neck, nose in the air, born to be admired. Hey, check these out, they seem to be saying.

Bison, on the other hand, are in tatters. They seem to take forever to change from winter to summer coats. They tear at the meadow hour upon hour, taking little evident note of peo-ple with cameras closing in on them. Occasionally, when visi-tors get too close, they charge without warning, inflicting bloody gorings. Visitors with video cameras have made films of other visitors flying through the air.

By late summer the river and the valley look weary, the grasses well munched and well trodden, the stream low and slow, often weedy at the surface. Some weeks before that I came upon a small herd of bison along the road, calves, cows, bulls young and old. There was a hollow rumbling among them, like the sound of distant thunder, and much rolling on the ground, feet in the air. At times, bulls stood head to head, a stance of the rut.

One old bull got caught up in a liberation movement when the three cows he was tending decided the grass was greener across the road. The trio started to cross, but as he headed off one, the others made progress, until two broke and ran across. Idling motors heated up, cars and RVs stretched out of sight; it looked like a stalled rush hour. Except that the only distemper here came from the snorting bull that was losing con-trol of his cows.

On word of hotter action to the west—reports of butting, stomping bulls raising clouds of dust—I set out on the Mary Mountain Trail. Along a rough ellipse of nine miles I saw, much buffalo sign and often stepped in it, but not a single ani-mal until I returned to the jammed road.

At twilight I drove up a spur road to the summit of 8,348-foot Lake Butte. Yellowstone Lake, spreading away to the south, had the look of an open sea. Wind fetched across it, beating waves against the shore bluffs, hissing through the trees. The cloud-veiled sun kindled a sheen on the lake, but there was no warmth in it. The horizon slowly closed in—the Gallatin Range fading in the northwest, the Tetons and the Red Mountains to the south. Wisps of steam marked the West Thumb Geyser Basin. Then they too vanished. Night and wind remained. Yellowstone has antidotes for traffic jams.

Mid-July brings a new coterie to the Hayden Valley road: fly-fishermen making the pilgrimage to the Yellowstone River. One morning I drove into the picnic area at the wildlife crossing of Buffalo Ford, where my companion had spotted a couple of familiar figures stretching into chest-high waders. John Basmajian, a nuclear engineer as well as a true believer in the bumper-sticker slogan—"A bad day's fishing is better'n the best day working"—had driven through the night from Richland, Washington.

Red Lang, after a career as a pilot—fighter, test, and corporate—had a retirement address in Albuquerque. Between June and October, he resided in Yellowstone country. Red wore a cap with the logo, "Bud Lilly's Trout Shop." The mutual friend who introduced us was Bud Lilly.

*C*ause célèbre in the campaign to protect grizzlies, the RV park at Fishing Bridge (opposite) remains open for business—its 350 sites accommodate more than 100,000 campers each season (below). Yellowstone planned to remove all facilities from this area of prime grizzly habitat. Local political pressure and protests from RV campers changed that plan. Some facilities will go, the RV park will stay—the only campground in Yellowstone run by a concessionaire.

PAUL CHESLEY/PHOTOGRAPHERS ASPEN

FOLLOWING PAGES: In the pink of evening a fork of Tantalus Creek glows at Norris Geyser Basin. Creek flow rises and falls with thermal activity, recalling the myth of thirsty King Tantalus. Receding waters tantalized him each time he bent to drink.

81

Bud has fished Yellowstone since 1935. His roots in the country go back to the 1860s, when an ancestor drove a load of telegraph wire into the area around Bozeman and caught the gold fever at Virginia City. He no longer owns the shop, but still retains the touch and the patience that made him one of the best known guides in the region.

Park officials told me it was the support of guides such as Bud Lilly that helped them transform a collapsed fishery into a sportsman's dream. The Greater Yellowstone Coalition, embracing envirmental groups across the ecosystem, offered a day of fishing with Bud for a thousand-dollar contribution. There had been nine takers when I joined him for an outing. We waded out just above Upper Falls, where a good mix of bottom vegetation offered cover to the cutthroat trout and a place for insects to hatch. The season said caddis flies and mayflies should be floating up to the surface; the drizzly day said not much would hatch until it warmed up. So Bud began with wet flies that resemble forms of the aquatic insects before they reach the surface. We also tried the woolly bugger, a version of the time-tested Yellowstone woolly worm. "It just looks like something good to eat," Lilly explained. But the cutthroat were fasting.

With late morning came a pause in the rain and a bit of warming. Bugs began to pop on the surface. Swallows swept up most of them; then a cutthroat rose and took one. Some of the insects floated by us. Mayflies. "Green Drake," Bud called, as he tied one on and with long graceful swoops presented it, a feathery landing just upstream of the action. A 16-inch cutthroat took the fly.

To a stranger on western waters the name cutthroat hints at meanness, a challenging foe. In fact, the name derives from the red streaks under the jaw. The brook, rainbow, and brown trout are wilier, tougher to land, the brown toughest of all.

And yet, if line, leader, and fly plop down in a heap, eight feet from where the caster flailed out, even the cutthroat knows what's up. That is not a fly. Only twice in two days did a cutthroat mistake my offerings for something good to eat. Those two changed their minds and slipped the hook. Not that it mattered; park catch-and-release policy forbids keepers on this part of the river.

Some anglers, Bud included, think the cutthroat has gotten smarter and meaner. Yet the "dumb gene," as biologist Bob Gresswell calls it, helps keep anglers happy. "It is the extreme gullibility of the native cutthroat trout," Gresswell wrote, "that makes them such a superb recreational resource." One study found that the average cutthroat is hooked about ten times a season; some fish were caught three times in a single day.

At one time Yellowstone resembled a fish farm, with hatcheries shipping cutthroat eggs and fry worldwide. By the 1960s the fishery was worn out, though some conservation

Steam rises from Grand Prismatic, largest of Yellowstone's thermal springs and one of the most colorful. Various microorganisms paint vivid rings in the 370-foot-wide pool. Certain bacteria contribute the orange and red hues. Vandals carved letters into the sinter and algal growth of one section (below). Park features can take years to recover from such abuse. Visitors who step off the boardwalks onto the thin, fragile crust of thermal features risk scalding— even death.

"When I'm in bear country, I recognize only two kinds of trees," jokes seasonal naturalist Barbara Pettinga, leading a hike in Hayden Valley, "those I can climb and those that I can't." Survivor of a grizzly attack some years ago, Barbara speaks from experience. For 11 summers she gave visitors "a bear's-eye view of Yellowstone."

had taken hold. In that decade the Park Service accepted a daunting challenge: to preserve natural processes in the parks "as nearly as possible in the condition that prevailed when the area was first visited by the white man." As Yellowstone moved toward that goal, fish as food for humans became a minor concern.

"We don't plan to give everyone a fish dinner," said Ron Jones, leader of the U.S. Fish and Wildlife Service project that manages the resource at Yellowstone. Gresswell was his assistant. "Our first priority is the fish. We protect them so that they can reproduce naturally. And we want enough of them so that they can furnish food for the other members of the ecosystem. Bears, otters, mink, ospreys, eagles, pelicans. The birds on Yellowstone Lake eat more than 300,000 pounds of fish a year. They're gonna get their fish. And then if we think we have a surplus, which in many populations we do, we let people keep fish."

Most roadside cutthroat streams, easily accessible, are catch and release only. Elsewhere the park sets a limit of two, and, in an intriguing flip-flop, keepers in the Yellowstone Lake area must be under 13 inches. Larger cutthroat make the best spawners; they are the lake's keepers. Thus arose the strange complaint: "I fished for hours before I hooked one small enough to keep." A bulging creel, however, is no longer the lure. Fly-fishing in Yellowstone is. Parkwide, more than half a million a year get hooked.

Ron Jones and I boated out to Clear Creek, a major spawning stream, to watch workers count the arriving cutthroat. The peak was July 12, 1987 when 6,388 funneled up the creek in a single day. Cutthroat have decreased to about half of their historical population since then—6,000 fish counted for the entire year 1994 and 15,000 in 1995. The culprit seems to be lake trout, a non-native species that preys on cutthroat, noticed first in 1994. Park fisheries biologists called in experts from the Great Lakes who had been studying the collapse of the lake trout fishery for some years to suggest how to eradicate what seems to be an exploding population—150 lake trout counted in 1995 and 900 in 1996—and yet restore cutthroats. Biologists have located a spawning ground near Carrington Island in Yellowstone Lake and have gill netted fish there. Meanwhile studies continue, supported in part by fishing license fees initiated in 1994.

One day at the Fish and Wildlife office I watched a videotape with microbiologist Tony Remsen. He and other members of a research team from the Center for Great Lakes Studies at the University of Wisconsin-Milwaukee had begun a major exploration of the bottom of Yellowstone Lake with a camera mounted on a roving submersible. Hot water vents and deep fissures appeared on the screen. Jets of sand shot up from little mounds. Bubbles popping up from the bottom gave the water the look of champagne. Bubbling with excitement at the unfolding visual treat, a scientist taping commentary exulted: "National Geographic, eat your heart out."

One major goal of the exploration is to determine the impact of geothermally heated groundwater on the relatively high growth of algae in the lake. Around the hot water vents scientists have observed life-forms based on chemosynthesis rather than photosynthesis—bacteria deriving energy from methane, sulfides, or sulfur rather than from the light of the sun. And in the depths of Yellowstone Lake, as in deep ocean clefts, there may be communities of organisms based solely on chemosynthesis. "For a microbiologist," mused Tony Remsen, "Yellowstone is like going to heaven. This is where you can see how bacteria and blue-green algae adapt to various properties of the hot springs and pools. This must be like the way things were a billion and a half or two billion years ago, before some of the higher forms of life evolved."

"I...had reather fight two Indians than one bear"

-Captain Meriwether Lewis in his journal, May 11, 1805

Back to higher forms of life. "The road between Canyon and Tower will be closed between 2000 this evening and 0800 Saturday." I heard the disquieting words from a park ranger's radio. They meant that Bear 104 and the cubs were about to be evicted from their roadside hangout on the flanks of Mount Washburn. Nobody wanted "another Bear 59." In October 1986 rangers had killed 59 near Canyon, when they found her on the partly eaten body of a photographer.

Around that time Bear 104, a 4½-year-old with cubs of the year, was hanging out just east of the park, feeding on clover, horse manure, and sewage at resort lodges. Aversive conditioning had been tried—a rubber bullet fired from a special gun, painful but not injurious. The "thumper" had some effect; she left the site where she took the hit. But she did not leave the area. The following spring she and the yearlings were moved to the Blacktail Deer Plateau, in the park's northern backcountry. She soon turned up at Washburn, one of the most popular hiking spots in Yellowstone.

I had hoped to see her off. Instead, with the road closed, I went off to dinner at the Lake Hotel, marveling at the contrasts of Yellowstone. Opened in 1891, Lake is the park's oldest operating hotel. Unlike the plain original, today's version, still in the process of transformation, is envisioned as Yellowstone's upscale flagship hotel. The new lobby, brightly pasteled and wickered, and the dining room, with its broad, carpeted entryway, have a Gatsbyesque air. F. Scott Fitzgerald might know these rooms.

Here one daydreams of white flannels and brass-buttoned blazers and straw boaters, of filmy dresses and cascading tresses and lighthearted laughter like music. Alas, only dreams. The wide-awake world is blue jeans and Bermudas. Here some friends and I sipped wine and dined on trout amandine and duck á l'orange and prime rib, and a string quartet played Mozart and Haydn and Borodin. Up the road, to the north, they were aiming a dart at 104.

It misfired. The tranquilizer failed to penetrate. Next day crowds converged at Mae West Curve, the road segment bending down from Mount Washburn above Antelope Creek. Here a six-armed ranger directed traffic, pointed out the

moving dots in a sage patch, and tried to head off the charge of the light-headed brigade—people marching downslope toward a mother grizzly and two cubs.

We watched through the glasses as 104 and the cubs sashayed to and fro through the sage and open grass. They were loose knit and close knit. At times one of the cubs would periscope, stiffening on hind legs, spot the sow, and beat it toward her. The cubs frisked among themselves and with their mother. She rolled one; I could see legs in the air. It broke off and ran. Closer now, the sow seemed to be turning rocks, searching for food. Golden saddle, golden sides, and when she turned away, a round, brown rump.

Visitors came and went, their Yellowstone day immensely enriched. The management team waited patiently. The next morning they found 104 along the road, fired a dart— and missed. Then they built a "scent trail," ranger Mike Bader told me, dragging a hind quarter of a road-killed moose from her vicinity to a cylindrical bear trap.

"She wouldn't go in," said Mike. "She was trap wise. So we locked Jamie Jonkel—he worked for the Interagency Grizzly Bear Study Team—into the trap with a dart gun and left the meat about ten yards away. When she came to it, he darted her." They put her into the trap, and soon the cubs came in. The trapdoor dropped, and off the trio went by helicopter to the southern backcountry.

There they survived a freak storm that blew down whole stands of trees in 1,000 acres of forest around them and in 14,000 acres more in adjoining Bridger-Teton National Forest. By late summer the bears had made their way back to the East Entrance area—some 25 mountainous miles. Again they were sighted, then disappeared. In the backcountry 104 managed to slip her radio collar off. If only she would stay in the wild . . . that was the hope, though the next year 104 remained near the East Entrance—but out of harm's way. The cubs were weaned two-year-olds, on their own, though probably not far off. She was trapped again in 1991 and had three two-year old cubs with her, and in December 1994 her radio collar stopped transmitting. Not many tales of roadside bears have happy endings, but this one might.

At the high end, suites at the Lake Hotel, Old Faithful Inn, and Mammoth Hot Springs Hotel run more than two hundred dollars a night. All have accommodations under $50 as well, and Roosevelt Lodge cabins go for as little as $22. Campgrounds are cheaper, and the backcountry, with a thousand miles of trails, is free.

There are three ultimate hikes in Yellowstone, says Ranger Rick Hutchinson: the Hoodoo Basin in the northeast, with the rugged badlands sculpture of the Absarokas; the Snake River region in the south, and east to the Thorofare country; and finally, the Bechler country of the southwest.

Rick knows where the wild raspberries grow. Rick knows where the sweet waters flow, the least likely to be tainted by *Giardia* protozoa. Such knowledge comes as a happy side effect of an infectious, incurable thermomania. I saw a symptom one day at Midway Geyser Basin, walking with him through the multicolored steam clouds of Grand Prismatic Spring. "I always heard there was a hell on earth," remarked a woman just ahead, in the thick of the miasma. "Hell?" Rick called out. "I think this is heaven." It is a bountiful heaven, with some 10,000 thermal features spread across the park. As geothermal specialist, Rick monitors them.

He was due for a look at some of the 465 hot springs

in the Bechler region. To the Bechler we went, Rick, photographer Raymond Gehman, and I, backpacking in from the west, then along Boundary Creek in the park sliver that lies in Idaho. We slept by a thermal field through a night of rain. My "miracle fabric" tent, designed to shed rain, miraculously took on the quality of our surroundings—the porous rhyolite layers of the Madison Plateau. A dripping backpacker tent, with no wriggle room, becomes a wilderness version of the Chinese water torture. In the morning we drew warmth from the hot springs, as we stood in luminous vapors beside runoff channels edged in yellow and orange and dark green.

This is the Cascade Corner of Yellowstone. Rain and snowmelt sieve through the rhyolite and spill down the steep edges of the Madison and Pitchstone Plateaus. In the 1920s promoters of irrigation projects sought to cut the Bechler corner from park jurisdiction. They failed, as park defenders highlighted the beauties here.

Our trail now led to some of them. Sheer and lacy, more cascade than waterfall, Silver Scarf Falls ripples down an incline for some 250 feet. At neighboring Dunanda the falls fall, plunging more than a hundred feet off a Boundary Creek shelf. Across the broad Bechler Meadows and up the Bechler River between the two plateaus, Ouzel Falls streams down a canyon wall. We camped a few miles farther, between Iris Falls upstream, Colonnade Falls downstream. Rick knows where to bed down with water music—in stereo.

*A*mid all its splendors, Yellowstone has made generous provision for human recreations, somewhat to the detriment of language. Couples long ago must have discovered the coziness of rotting lodgepoles, and "rotten-logging" entered the vocabulary. So also with "hot-potting," soaking in streams warmed by thermal waters. Even before the park was born, squatters set up spas around Mammoth Hot Springs. Although bathing in thermal features is forbidden, soaking in some streams is still allowed.

We took the waters on the Bechler's Ferris Fork. A hot spring bubbled up in midstream; nearby a cold-water spring poured in. As you like it: hot or cold or both, one shoulder basting, the other shivering. It was all play until Dunbar Susong came along with work to do. The veteran area ranger carried a snorkel and chain, hoping to dislodge a boulder that had partly blocked the hot water opening. Several times he dove to the vent; the heat forced him back. Finally he got the chain in place, formed us into a chain gang, and Yo, Heave, Ho we went, dumping backward, some into hot water, some into cold. At last the rock yielded, and Dunbar's backcountry Baden-Baden once more flowed unfettered.

Dunbar and a group of rangers from nearby Targhee National Forest had ridden horses in. We went over for breakfast one freezing morning to find the Targhee rangers at a portable stove, stamping their feet and muttering. I knew some

of them, had seen them ride through rougher, colder days high in the Tetons. What got them muttering here was all the dead-wood around, and no crackling blaze to fight the morning chill. But a no-wood-fire policy at heavily used campsites minimizes the impact of backcountry visitors. The Targhee rangers, a bit hoarse and drippy nosed, formed an informal choir and warmed us with a plaintive refrain: "Put another lahhhg on the fi-uhr."

We laughed and ate, thanked the Targhee men for the fine cuisine and Dunbar for the fine Bechler country. We packed out, taking two days to hike 11 miles, the weary conclusion of a 36-mile trek.

Someone asked Jim Bridger, the mountain man and tale spinner, if he had ever seen the stone trees of the Southwest, so the story goes. Old Gabe started spinning. "O, that's peetrifac-tion. Come with me to the Yellowstone next summer, and I'll show you peetrified trees a-growing, with peetrified birds on 'em a-singing peetrified songs."

Forget the stone birds. The trees stopped growing some 50 million years before Bridger set a trap in Yellowstone, when ash and debris burst from volcanoes and lava flowed, burying the forests and in time turning the wood to stone. The stone trees

are scattered across 24½ square miles. Unlike the fallen, drifted trees of Arizona's petrified forest, many here still stand. Today's living forest, high and cold, is awesome in size, never in variety—a few pine, fir, and spruce species, even fewer leafy ones, aspen, willow, cottonwood.

The forest of 50 million years ago grew on rolling land several thousand feet lower than today's 7,000-foot-high plateaus; from the petrified remains scientists have identified a variety of species that are found today in much warmer climates. In Yellowstone grew dogwood and magnolia, oak and maple, hickory and walnut. They may have grown in different forests at different times. A study in one area concluded that 27 successive forests were buried, one above the other.

John Good, former chief naturalist of the park, enjoying a busy retirement, offered to show me some specimens on Specimen Ridge. This long cliff, rising 1,200 feet in the north of the park, sends waters down to the Lamar River from creeks named Crystal and Jasper, Opal and Amethyst and Chalcedony. One embellishment of Bridger's tale had petrified flowers blooming "in colors of crystal." We never found them. We turned uphill near Crystal Creek and had to make do with the living—snow and shrubby cinquefoil, lupine, monkshood, yellow salsify, and fringed gentian, Yellowstone's official flower.

After a sweaty climb—"steeper'n a cow's face," claimed John—to the ridge crest, we found more flowers: tiny yellow blooms that had somehow found nurture atop the stump of a stone redwood. The stump measures 26 ½ feet around; just below it, on a narrow finger of rock, rise two pines, taller and thinner than the redwood. They were stained and cracked, diverging slightly—a peetrified victory sign high on Specimen Ridge.

No rush on the down leg. Much about Yellowstone is wondrous, unique; the valley of the Lamar River on this day struck me as simply beautiful. The valley has no roadside spectaculars, such as those of the geyser basins; the valley road was uncrowded. We looked out on rock and grass and sage and the swell of late-spring bloom, at patches of conifer, streams descending, low knobs and benches and high parapets—the valley, in scale, containing all, harmonizing all in a mosaic of Rocky Mountain grandeur.

O sborne Russell, the fur trapper, wrote oft-quoted words of tribute to the Lamar, his Secluded Valley: "I almost wished I would spend the remainder of my days in a place like this where happiness and contentment seemed to reign in wild romantic splendor." In the 1840s Russell, who read Shakespeare and the Bible in camp, sadly concluded that it was time "to leave the mountains as Beaver and game had nearly disappeared." A century later rangers were rounding up "surplus" elk in Secluded Valley, shipping them off or killing them. John Good remembers the 1960s.

"We had an elk trap here," he said as we strolled a rise

"the Buffaloe is already a stranger"

–Osborne Russell
Journal of a Trapper (1834-1843)

Dust billows around a bison taking a midsummer roll in Yellowstone's broad Hayden Valley—to rid itself of insects perhaps. The park herd, a remnant of millions of bison that once roamed North America, now numbers about 3,500. Bison sometimes stray beyond park boundaries; cattlemen fear the spread of brucellosis, a bovine disease endemic in the herd. Montana law directs that bison straying from the park be captured and slaughtered. More than 400 animals were destroyed during the winter of 1995-96 when they left the protection of the park in search of food.

*G*aze golden and unblinking, a great gray owl scouts prey in Yellowstone. In more active pursuit of food, a coyote bounds through tall meadow grasses. Miles away at Sheepeater Cliffs, where these rodents often join human picnickers, a yellow-bellied marmot scratches contentedly in the summer sun. The wild vastness of the Yellowstone ecosystem shelters a wide variety of animals large and small.

near Crystal Creek. "It was a huge corral with loading pens. Wing fences ran maybe half a mile away from the entrance. Helicopters would round up the elk and herd them in. It was fantastic to watch. Then of course the rangers would close in and we would load the animals on trucks. They would be transported to Montana and Wyoming and put on ranges where they could be hunted.

"And we were shooting the same way. We used helicopters to round up the elk to shoot them. It wasn't very pleasant. We would bring them into a mass, and then the rangers would start shooting into them until all the elk were dead. We had professional butchers who would gut the animals out." The carcasses went for food, to Indian reservations and schools.

By 1969 the northern elk herd—one of eight in Yellowstone—numbered 4,300. Under the policy of preserving natural processes in the parks, nature—now harsh, now gentle—regulates the herd size. Wolves, coyotes, cougars, black bears, and grizzlies pick off some of the young and the halt. Outside the park, of course, hunters continue to take a toll of those that migrate.

B y the late 1990s, after several mild winters, the northern elk herd population has swelled to around 30,000. Range scientists from surrounding states, long critical of natural regulation, warned of serious deterioration of the northern range, where the herd seeks forage in winter. Elk, one scientist told me, go to less desirable forages when their favored grasses run low; this depletes the food supplies of other animals and can permanently degrade the range. The answer, from his point of view, is a return to the old ways, along with an education program to gain public acceptance of occasional slaughters.

John Varley, Yellowstone's chief of research, replied: There is no evidence of range damage because of overgrazing; the northern range holds the same mix of flora today as it did when the elk numbered 4,000. Yet questions persist. The park has sought answers in scores of research projects related to the northern range.

The gray wolf once again joins the cougar to help in the natural regulation of elk. Under the old Park Service policy of manipulating wildlife numbers, Yellowstone long ago killed off the wolves and the mountain lions. There may be upwards of 20 mountain lions resident on the northern range. Perhaps some cougars survived in Yellowstone; others have moved in from north of the park. Occasionally a wolf sighting was reported. It may have been a coyote. Or it may have indeed been a wolf. But a lone wolf did not make a population. A wolf pack hadn't hunted in Yellowstone since the 1920s. The ecosystem lacked a major component, an endangered species in the lower 48 except in Minnesota.

Environmental groups across the nation, notably Defenders of Wildlife, joined in a crusade to bring the wolves back. In accordance with the Endangered Species Act, the U.S.

"I wish to speak a word for Nature for absolute freedom and wildness"

–Henry David Thoreau
"Walking," 1862

Fish and Wildlife Service submitted a recovery plan in 1994 seeking to establish ten breeding pairs. The recovery area centers on 8.5 million acres, including Yellowstone, surrounding national forest wilderness, and undeveloped wildlands; it envisioned protection not only for the wolf but also for the interests of livestock owners and others. With so much space and so much prey in Yellowstone, biologists felt that overall there was little danger of serious conflict.

The Park Service welcomed the plan, but members of Congress from the surrounding states tried to block it; ranchers were not impressed by the built-in protections of the plan. They wanted the right to dispatch a wolf that threatened their property. Current law makes it a crime for a private citizen to kill an animal of an endangered species. A 1982 amendment could allow exceptions. One rancher told me he wanted the law changed "so that any wolf that so much as sets foot outside of Yellowstone is dead, even in wilderness and any other public land."

Those are the shepherd's ancient fears. Beyond them, there are also the fairy-tale fears of Red Riding Hood, defying all indications that in the real world wolves do not prey on humans. Despite the obstacles, proponents did not lost hope, and the first wolves, captured in Canada, were released in January 1995 with a second batch released in 1996. There is a following across the land for the wolf in Yellowstone. The ranchers' concerns are respected.

Northeast of Yellowstone Lake, the helicopter settled on a bit of cleared slope of the 9,600-foot-high volcanic blip, and we quickly unloaded jugs of fresh water to resupply Kerry Gunther, then the grizzly watcher of Pelican Cone. He may have been the most isolated graduate student in the land. He awaited us beside the hut, $13\frac{1}{2}$ by $13\frac{1}{2}$ feet, with upper walls of glass, that served as his summer hermitage for most of five summers.

From the door bear bells hung. By the bed stood a 12-gauge shotgun. There was another seasonal dwelling a hundred yards away, and when Kerry arrived each spring, the snows still deep, he checked to see if anyone was home. And breathed a sigh of relief to find it empty. It was a hollow under tree roots, a grizzly's winter den.

His pinups were grizzlies. "Keeps my mind on my work," he said. "Real pinups might be the worst thing I could have for this job." From May 15 until July 4, when the Pelican Valley Trail opened to hikers, the 29-year-old biologist recorded more than a hundred sightings of grizzlies but saw not a single human being. On stormy days he sees nothing beyond the glass walls; he could write a thesis on cabin fever.

He watched through binoculars and a telescope that can resolve a bear at seven miles. His major focus in the 12,000 acres of open meadow within the Pelican Creek drainage, a prime grizzly habitat, was to see whether humans affect bear use of the valley. The data that went into his thesis at Montana State University have helped the park manage the human traffic. Up to a fifth of Yellowstone is closed or restricted at various times in the interests of the grizzly.

Early morning mist swirls across an island in the Yellowstone River, obscuring the Hayden Valley beyond. On the lookout for a meal, a raptor perches in a flood-killed lodgepole pine.

FOLLOWING PAGES: Sunrise pierces a grove of lodgepole pines as waterfowl paddle near Fishing Bridge over the Yellowstone River. Once a favorite fishing area, this bridge near the outlet of Yellowstone Lake attracted thousands of anglers each summer. To protect spawning trout and to restore fish populations, the park banned fishing here in 1973.

Kerry's data make clear that grizzlies that have not become habituated to humans avoid them. When hikers or horsemen were in the valley, Kerry saw fewer bears and those stayed closer to cover. At times he has seen hikers and a grizzly on a collision course. Miles away, he could do nothing but watch. One day three backpackers came up a trail, heads down, to within 25 yards of a young grizzly. The leader saw the bear and stopped, the others hiked straight on into the leader; then all backtracked. A half hour later, the scene was replayed: The lead backpacker froze, the others collided, then all circled around. The bear stayed. Soon a bull bison came along. This time the bear ran off.

In May, elk are dropping calves in Pelican, and grizzlies enjoy fresh meat. "When the calves are real young," said Kerry, "the bears can just walk fast and knock them over." By June, when the calves can run, hunting success slips to 50 percent, the chase ending when the grizzly cuts inside of a turning calf and swats it down. When I visited Kerry in September 1987, Pelican Valley had turned brown, the grasses too dry for grizzlies. The bears were mostly out of sight, digging up caches of whitebark pine nuts in the woodlands.

Kerry had known bleak times here. Now, as the season of isolation waned, he brushed them aside and thought instead of his exceptional vantage point. From his perch atop the volcanic peak he had spotted grizzlies more than a thousand times, saw them confront humans, chase down elk. "Not too many people get to watch that," Kerry concluded.

Below the cone Pelican Creek flows south, then west, emptying into Yellowstone Lake near Fishing Bridge. "That national park slum called Fishing Bridge," said a Conservation Foundation report on the parks in 1967.

The log trestle bridge, across the Yellowstone River where it flows out of the lake, makes a fine vantage for watching the spawning run of cutthroat. The fisherman jams of yesteryear are gone. It's not the bridge, but the neighborhood of the same name that draws fire. Here, on one side of the East Entrance Road are a visitor center and a park campground; on the other a concessionaire spread of general store, photo shop, gas station, and a facility for recreational vehicles, the only one in the park with full hookups, the only one privately operated.

As at Canyon, there's no tenting at Fishing Bridge. For the same reason: grizzly bears. With the park's momentous turn to natural regulation at the end of the 1960s, grizzlies no longer had the pick of 40,000 pounds of garbage each day during the summer. The dumps were closed, the grizzlies forced to depend on natural food. Those who wouldn't and scavenged campgrounds—as many had done even with open dumps—would finally get ridden out of Yellowstone, or destroyed; scores of grizzlies were lost to the park this way.

A viable population, park managers contended, would remain in the wild. But grizzlies continue to visit people places, including the Fishing Bridge area. In the decade beginning in 1977 grizzlies dropped by 77 times. Fishing Bridge contributed to the destruction of eight bears, the transfer of nine others. Another study showed that of every five human injuries caused by grizzlies around a development, three occurred in the Fishing Bridge vicinity.

*T*he area is natural grizzly country, a convergence of desirable habitat along the lakeshore, the river, and Pelican Valley. In the early 1970s Yellowstone decided to close the development and build new lodging facilities in Grant Village on the West Thumb of Yellowstone Lake. The new lodgings opened in the early '80s—a cluster of modernistic buildings, pinkish and brown, reminiscent of raw developments on the frontiers of suburbia. The accommodations seem adequate; but for many in Yellowstone it is yet another scar on the landscape. "I don't go to Grant Village," one ranger told me. "I regard it as an obscenity, the most obtrusive development on the lakeshore." The lodgings at Grant Village opened, but Fishing Bridge did not close. The latter is the park's closest development to Cody, Wyoming, and town merchants did not want it closed. Recreational vehicle owners across the land, according to then Park Superintendent Robert Barbee, did not want the vehicle park closed. U.S. Senator Alan Simpson, of Cody, did not want Fishing Bridge facilities removed.

A park staff report in 1984 warned that the cumulative effect of operating both facilities was potentially "disastrous"

Veteran angler Bud Lilly has cast in Yellowstone waters for more than half a century. With a flick of the wrist, he drops line and fly into a likely pool on the Yellowstone River. "It just looks like something good to eat," he says of the intricate flies he uses to attract cutthroat and other trout. One of the area's best known guides, Bud ties flies to match insects that are hatching at fishing time. Park regulations often require fishermen to release their catch; the lure lies more in hooking the fish than in keeping them.

for the grizzly. A few years later, a 300-page environmental impact study, with cumulative-effects computer modeling, found that grizzlies might benefit if the park campground at Fishing Bridge were removed and other steps taken to avoid confrontations. The study proposed that a new campground be built elsewhere on the lake. The RV park and the visitor center could stay.

Environmental groups, having fought Fishing Bridge for years, denounced the proposal. A newsletter of the Yellowstone Park Preservation Council—many of whose members work in the park—portrayed the issue as "a battle between those who want the park managed for the future and those who would manage it as a tourist trap." The decision, said the council, was shaped under the influence of Senator Simpson and the "special interest groups" he represented. A spokesperson for Simpson maintained that the senator had an obligation to his constituency. "If constituents are special interests then he's proud to represent those special interests in the process. The park was created as a pleasuring ground for the people. It is not wilderness and should not be managed as such."

After thousands of letters poured in, the park decided to begin a parkwide campsite reservation system and defer construction of a new campground. The old campground and the photo shop closed in 1990, while the gas station remains open. "If we had the best of all worlds," Robert Barbee told me, "we would have removed all the facilities from Fishing Bridge. That was not to be."

Since the mid-1970s the grizzlies of Greater Yellowstone have been designated as threatened, and a recovery plan has operated under the Endangered Species Act. The program establishes priority for the bears over human activities in critical grizzly habitat. Population totals are difficult to come by. By one estimate some 300 grizzlies use six million acres of key habitat in Greater Yellowstone. According to Richard Knight, who heads the Interagency Grizzly Bear Study Team, important keys to recovery are a permanent guarantee of natural habitat and a limit on human-caused grizzly deaths. The survival of adult females is especially crucial. "We've reached a 92 percent survival rate," he said, "and we need to maintain 92 percent forever." Overall, the recovery trend in the 1980s has been slightly uphill, observed Knight. Going back to 1970, however, "we're still slightly downhill."

Northwest of Fishing Bridge the land itself has its ups and downs. When the earth's crust flexes up at the lake's northern end, the water overflows the southeastern shoreline. "It's like jacking up one leg of a bathtub," said Wayne Hamilton, research geologist for the park. Strange things happen.

Ken Diem, past director of the National Park Service-University of Wyoming Research Center, studied—from 1949 until his retirement in 1986—a white pelican colony on two tiny islets in a southeastern arm of the lake. In years of record spring runoff enough ground remained above water for a successful nesting. Then one season, with runoff high but no record breaker, Diem found the adults of one islet standing in water, the nestlings drowned.

In 1974, geophysicist Robert Smith of the University of Utah was conducting seismic profiles of the lake basin. "I could see the lake-bottom sediments tilted back from the north to the south," he recalled. The lake waters flow south to north, emptying into the river at Fishing Bridge. Smith wondered, "How can you have sediments dipping this way, when the lake drainage goes the other way?"

To get some answers, the U.S. Geological Survey undertook to resurvey the benchmarks placed along the park roads in 1923. Made in the mid-seventies, the new readings were studied at the University of Utah. "They astonished everybody," said Smith. Part of the Yellowstone caldera had risen. At Le Hardy Rapids, a few miles north of Fishing Bridge, the rise was 740 millimeters, more than two feet, an average of more than a half inch per year. Active volcanic regions record such numbers. "Remarkable rates," Smith observed. The uplift continued, even increased. A Geological Survey study in 1985 revealed a reversal; the ground started to subside.

By the end of 1987 scientists had a pile of data from surveys, laser beam readings, seismic soundings, gravity measurements, and orbiting satellites of the Global Positioning System. The evidence that had been analyzed indicated the land deformation could be caused by unusual hydrothermal activity, increased tectonic activity, or the movement of some partly melted rock perhaps three to five miles below the surface. The likely location lies north of Fishing Bridge and Le Hardy Rapids. Professor Smith believes the semimolten rock has a mushy texture, like oatmeal and cream perhaps, heated from a source some 60 miles below it.

What about future volcanic activity? "There's no reason to think that volcanism in Yellowstone is going to stop," says Smith. "There are quite likely to be further eruptions. The form that could take could be an eruption like those in Hawaii, spectacular but very small. It could be a larger one, but not catastrophic. And of course the ultimate could be an explosive eruption. The time frame of these things is unknown. The park is interested in our work—are we going to have a big volcanic eruption? I tell them it's unlikely in our lifetime. In the meantime there are going to be lots of earthquakes, many small ones and an occasional large one."

*T*he lake: about 136 square miles, with a "thumb" and three "arms"; always cold at the surface, boiling in places on the bottom, its mood and aspect changing with the seasons. From the lounge of the Lake Hotel, awash with summer sunshine, the twinkling vista invites the eye to hazy, distant mountain horizons. On a still, gray day in January, the frozen expanse reminded me of the poet Yankev Fridman's image: "God's breath, more silent than the breath of stars over sleeping wintertime lakes."

To a canoeist, first impressions do not inspire poetry:

FOLLOWING PAGES: "Now I know what it is to sit enthroned amid the clouds of sunset," exclaimed English writer Rudyard Kipling of the Grand Canyon of the Yellowstone River. Viewed from Artist Point, the Lower Falls plunges 308 feet into the great gorge. The Lower and the 109-foot Upper Falls, a little farther upstream, indicate where hard rhyolite, a lava rock layered in the broad Yellowstone caldera, yields to rhyolite altered by exposure to hot water and steam. Heat transforms the rhyolite, making it more easily eroded by the rushing water and changing its brown and gray hues to the yellows, whites, and reds of the precipitous canyon walls and pinnacles.

𝒱enting steam veils geothermal specialist Rick Hutchinson as he skirts a hot

spring on a hike with the author in the Bechler backcountry. To Rick, "this is heaven."

a big, cantankerous piece of water, ugly and threatening when the wind chops it up. "Ugly and threatening" wiped out the first day of a late-summer trip photographer Raymond Gehman and I had planned with John Good, Jeff Hardesty, and Julie Holding and Len Carlman, all up from Jackson, all active in the conservationist community.

Overnight, the lake calmed. To make up for lost time, we engaged a powerboat to ferry us from Bridge Bay Marina to the Promontory, the peninsula separating the South and Southeast Arms. Launching at the headland, we paddled down the confined, friendly waters of the Southeast Arm. Ospreys, sortieing from tree nests, shrieked an unwelcome.

From our camp at the end of the arm, we hiked rain-soaked meadow and a jungle gym of downed, slippery lodgepole. John and I made for the Trail Creek ranger cabin, which he remembered from his days as chief naturalist. "I wonder if the screen door is still on backwards," he remarked. Once when he arrived at the cabin, mosquitoes covered the door. And when it opened inward, they joined him. The cabin, a historical structure, has been carefully refurbished. But the screen door still opens backward.

Starting back, John sat down on a log and gazed across the arm to the Absaroka barrier. Rain pelted down. John stayed. "You know," he said, "I love every part of Yellowstone, some more than others. I hate to leave. I'm not sure I'm ever going to get back here."

With a clearing day we went canoe birding, swinging out a mile or so to the Molly Islands, where the famed white pelican colony nests. The islets, tiny mounds of sand and volcanic boulders, had the usual look of a breeding colony, whitened rocks and rotting bodies, and a bustle of adults and fledged young, all soon to head south for the winter. This is the site where the islet was drowned one year by the land rising to the north. It is the only white pelican nesting colony in a national park. In the 1920s the authorities, favoring human fishermen over pelicans and suspecting the birds of carrying a parasite harmful to trout, began destroying eggs and nestlings here. Then policies changed. In the '50s, when buzzing motorboats threatened the colony, motors were banned; today these are paddle-only waters.

From the islets we paddled southeast to the broad, flat delta where the lake receives the Yellowstone River. On a shrubby shore, alive with whirring songbirds, we identified—by waffling consensus—white-crowned and Lincoln's sparrows and yellow warblers. In and around and above the water, a trove: gadwalls, wigeons, goldeneyes, shoals of Canada geese, sandpipers, a harrier, a golden eagle. Later, at camp, we heard the hollow trumpeting of sandhill cranes. Loons settled on the arm; a faint cackling haunted the lakeshore.

Beating upwind, cracking ice in the water bottles at dawn, huddling at the fire with sodden socks and long johns steaming—this country, John Good was saying, makes you aware of fundamentals. Which way the wind blows matters. Overcast matters; only the sun will dry the tents.

One evening we paddled to a nearby meadow where a bull elk and his harem had been spotted. The rut had begun; with luck we might see the bull or another trumpeting defiance across the September night, the neck massive rather than graceful in this season, the rack high, velvet scrubbed off, and the antlers like candelabra in a moon near the full.

At the forest edge we waited, whispering, testing each footfall as night closed in. Then from our left came a kind of lowing, whining, roaring. And from the right a short, hollow growl. Then back and forth, the long, haunting passage and the growling response. More than two voices I thought. We hoped an open-field confrontation would climax the bugling, but it never came. Jeff Hardesty cracked dead wood against tree trunks to mimic the sound of a bull banging his antlers against trees. Perhaps it would chum up a curious challenger. No luck. A few cows ventured into the meadow, nibbled, stared toward us, faded from view.

We left the primal symphony and retraced our route to the shore. Under the open sky we paddled slowly back, afloat on a lake of rippling ebony, entranced by a gibbous moon hung high above the mountains.

So it ends. A Yellowstone spring and summer. Elk and grizzlies and bison, cutthroat and pelicans, the stone trees above the Lamar, the water music of the Bechler, the sunlit steam clouds along the Firehole, the moon-streaked lake—I hear you John Good. I hate to leave.

Soldier-straight lodgepole pine—killed by mountain beetles—catch sunset's

glow. Standing dead trees such as these, called snags, fueled the wildfires of 1988.

*S*erene waters of the Southeast Arm of Yellowstone Lake invite quiet canoeing. White pelicans wing toward island rookeries. Pelicans in the park have produced as many as 400 young. While the park bans visitors from the nesting islands, nests are not safe from occasional floods such as the high water in 1996 that reduced the number of chicks to fledge to three.

FOLLOWING PAGES: *Living symbol of man's uneasy association with the wildlife of Yellowstone National Park, a bison bull ambles across the Lamar Valley road.*

The Fires of 1988

S o much burned, for so long, racing with the winds in wild, untamable bursts across the bone-dry summer of 1988. Is it still wonderland? Fires spread over some 990,000 acres in Yellowstone Park, emptying campgrounds and housing, vaulting over Old Faithful. In surrounding national forests about 420,000 acres burned, including parts of the North Absaroka, Teton, and Absaroka-Beartooth Wildernesses.

It does not take long, entering the park, say, from West Yellowstone, Montana, driving east along the Madison River, to see Shakespeare's haunting line writ large: "Bare ruin'd choirs where late the sweet birds sang." Black quills rise from ashes; a forest floor that scarcely knew sunlight is now awash with it. Nor does it take long before the ghost forest yields to a green one, lightly singed or not at all, and then to meadows parched and meadows untouched. In the flames' wake wildlife meandered across the crazy quilt. Grizzlies feasted on fire-killed elk and gathered insects from burned snags. In October, while parts of Yellowstone country still smoldered, elk grazed meadows, black and tan, along the Madison. Bulls screeched their autumnal longings and rubbed antlers against charred saplings, scraping them white.

Through the gaping fire scars new vistas appeared: cave openings, canyon walls, waterfalls. The lodgepole forest, a green monotony, made few hearts flutteróuntil it burned. Now some visitors sighed at skeletal boles: Our grandchildren will never see the Yellowstone we knew. Yet tomorrow's Yellowstone may be richer, more diverse in plant life. Aspen, highly prized and long in decline, may get a new lease on life. A century ago one park observer noted how aspen was "the first tree to spring up upon recently burned areas."

"Few areas had lethal soil heating below one to two inches," said park soil scientist Henry Shovic. "All the ecology that was aboveground is resident in the soil. Roots, rhizomes, seeds are sitting there, ready to repopulate the area. In springtime the ash becomes a fertilizer."

Above all, the Yellowstone that brought explorers and scientists, that inspired artists and tale spinners, remains intact. The geysers and mud pots and fumaroles and springs boil on. The Grand Canyon, color-enhanced by subterranean heat, largely escaped the fires. Hayden Valley, with its birds and fishes and bison and elk, escaped entirely.

There are invisible scars around Yellowstone, scars of mind and spirit. People who watched the flames brush by their homes believe that management of the fires endangered them; they do not believe official statements to the contrary. "There's no trust when they tell things to people who live around here and have eyes to see otherwise," said one resident of West Yellowstone. "You cannot sit in Washington and understand the mental devastation," said a Wyoming man

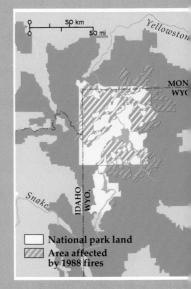

National park land

Area affected by 1988 fires

Black Saturday, August 20; Red-wreathed fireballs crackle through lodgepole pines near Norris in Yellowstone Park. Driven by a dry cold front with mile-a-minute gusts, the area fires fanned across 160,000 acres—spanning in a single day more than a tenth of the total area swept during the five-month fire season. The map (above) shows the 1.4 million acres of two parks and nearby forests that were affected by the fires.

FOLLOWING PAGES: Cold-front winds of September whip the North Fork Fire toward Old Faithful. Firebrands flew over the geyser to set ablaze the hill in the foreground, where the photographers stood. Crews snuffed embers that fell on Old Faithful Inn.

LARRY MAYER/*BILLINGS GAZETTE* (OPPOSITE)
ALAN AND SANDY CAREY (FOLLOWING PAGES)

119

Bathing a West Thumb cabin with fire-resistant foam (opposite, lower), holding a fence line at Norris (below)—fire fighters at developed areas scored notable victories in defense of life and property. But when the fires ran full bore through meadow and forest, fighters fought in vain.

A retardant drop (opposite) on a blazing hillside, "might as well have been gasoline," one observer said. The fire-fighting force in Greater Yellowstone, including soldiers, airmen, and marines, peaked at 9,500 in the first week of September; the cost neared 120 million dollars. One man died in the battle; more than 60 structures burned. Only rain and snow reversed the flaming tide. Lightning ignited most of the major fires; a cigarette set off the North Fork blaze.

forced to flee his fine ranch home on the Clarks Fork.

Yellowstone and Grand Teton and the national forests in varying degrees accept natural fire as a component of the ecosystem—so long as it does not threaten life or property or private land. Yellowstone officials insist that they never sacrificed safety in the interests of ecology. Reviewing the data, some experts found that there were clear signals of a potentially hot fire season by the end of June, weeks before the park abandoned natural burning. Other analysts agree with the park that no known strategy could have curbed the 1988 fires. In preceding years midsummer rains kept forest fires in check; '88 witnessed the driest summer on record. At least six dry cold fronts swept through, whipping the blazes ahead.

On September 7—"Ash Wednesday," the day the North Fork Fire jumped Old Faithful—park rangers Bill Blake and Hugh Dougher took a busman's holiday. Blake, of Yosemite, and Dougher, of Voyageurs Park, had been helping at fire command in West Yellowstone. They had seen the sky glow and went for a closer look. On the Grand Loop between Norris and Mammoth they came upon a boiling black cloud that spewed huge balls of fire. To their left a solid sheet of flame suddenly rose. "The fire started moving up and down the ridge," Blake recalled, "burning in a vortex—just like a tornado, but solid fire. The noise was maddening. It hurt our ears. It was the booming of tree hitting tree. The tornado was sucking air in and pulling up trees by the root balls, knocking them into each other like dominoes." According to Forest Service fire behavior analyst Robert Mutch, the two rangers witnessed a "double-burn phenomenon." In 1976 an intense fire had swept the ridge. Now the deadwood of the old burn was helping fuel a fire storm, with blazing whirls generating their own whirlwinds.

In its 116-year history, Yellowstone Park had known nothing like the summer of '88, and the political storms did

not die with the fires. There were biting allusions to Nero fiddling and, in contrast, hopeful visions of a Yellowstone phoenix rising, green and vigorous. The unprecedented size and ferocity of the fires, and the public outcry that followed, triggered a broad review of the natural-burn policy. Few sought a return to the discarded policy of suppressing all fires; it allowed a buildup of forest fuels and skewed the natural processes of the ecosystem. "We need a course of action," said park officials, "that will permit us to appreciate fire's place and power without so wholly risking the financial and emotional disasters of the 1988 fire season."

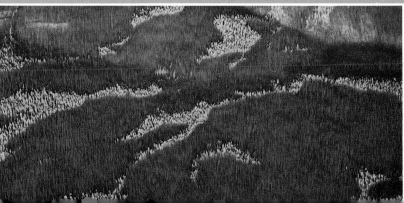

124

*A*utumn reprise: Elk reclaim Madison River habitat, grazing unburned meadow. An aerial view (opposite) reveals fire's vagabond ways in a patchwork of blackened masses, singed streaks, and untouched green islets. A seep nurtures sedges (right) in a fiercely burned patch. For the most part, wildlife seemed to take the flames in stride, and the earth started to renew itself almost immediately. Scientists have taken the opportunity to study the fire's impact on the Greater Yellowstone Ecosystem, initiating more than 250 research projects.

GRAND TETON

NATIONAL PARK

Summer into Autumn

Yellowstone National Park is primarily a region of volcanic plateaus," wrote the mountaineer geologist Friti of Fryxell in 1938, "and it is not here that the grandeur of the Rocky Mountains finds highest expression. For this, a Yellowstone traveler must look to the south." To the Tetons."There is magic in the name, and contagion." Fryxell caught the contagion as a doctoral researcher in Jackson Hole. He spread it as the first naturalist of Grand Teton National Park, as a pioneering Teton climber with 19 first ascents, and with the power and grace of his words.

Yellowstone was but a few months old when its first superintendent, Nathaniel P. Langford, looked south; in July 1872 Langford explored the Tetons and claimed that "after ten hours of the severest labor of my life," he and James Stevenson "stepped upon the highest point of the Grand Teton." If so, that would make them the first on record to stand on that cold, snow-seamed rock pile. Rivals for the honor and some of the leading Teton mountaineers of later days have disputed Langford's claim. Let the experts say what they will; that part about the laboring has the ring of truth to any tenderfoot who has lathered out on the untender ridges of the Grand.

Horace Albright, superintendent of Yellowstone during the 1920s, looked south again and again as he sought to expand his domain around the Teton spires—"the best part of Yellowstone . . . not yet in the park." But the Forest Service and ranchers—cattle and dude—had already laid claim to the mountains and the adjacent valley of Jackson Hole. Unlike its famous neighbor, which emerged full blown as the world's first national park with a sweeping national consensus, Grand Teton National Park gained its current status piecemeal, across long decades, in an agony of controversy.

"We're the most bastardized park in the system," said Marshall Gingery, then assistant superintendent for research and resource management. "We got a late start and we're playing catch-up." Grand Teton is a national park with its largest lake—Jackson Lake—dammed for irrigation of Idaho farms, with a commercial airport, with a major highway, and with dude ranching and cattle grazing.

The park even irrigates grazing land, in an arrangement that removed the livestock from a popular visitor area. By law the park is obliged to help keep in check the size of the Jackson elk herd; each fall hunters deputized as park rangers attempt to "harvest" the requisite numbers as the animals migrate down from their high summer range. Some of the elk, observers say, may shun the hunting ground during their migration to the adjacent National Elk Refuge—which also schedules a hunt as part of the elk reduction program. After the scheduled hunt ends, the entire refuge becomes a winter sanctuary.

Within the park boundaries lie more than 103 privately owned tracts, varying in size from a tenth of an acre to 400 acres. The park has nine on-site concessionaires—three times as many as Yellowstone—and it allows activities, such

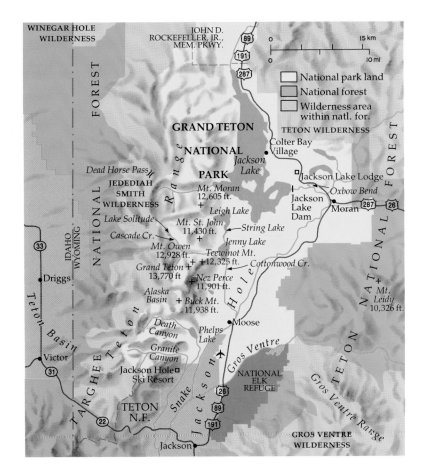

WINEGAR HOLE
WILDERNESS

JOHN D.
ROCKEFELLER, JR.,
MEM. PKWY.

National park land
National forest
Wilderness area
within natl. for.

GRAND TETON
NATIONAL
PARK

TETON WILDERNESS

Colter Bay
Village

Jackson
Lake

Jackson Lake Lodge

Dead Horse Pass
JEDEDIAH
SMITH
WILDERNESS

Mt. Moran
12,605 ft.

Oxbow Bend

Jackson
Lake
Dam

Moran

Lake Solitude
Cascade Cr.

Leigh Lake

Mt. St. John
11,430 ft.

String Lake

Jenny Lake

Mt. Owen
12,928 ft.

Teewinot Mt.
12,325 ft.

Cottonwood Cr.

Grand Teton
13,770 ft

Nez Perce
11,901 ft.

Alaska
Basin

Buck Mt.
11,938 ft.

Mt.
Leidy
10,326 ft.

Death
Canyon

Phelps
Lake

Moose

Granite
Canyon

Jackson Hole
Ski Resort

NATIONAL
ELK
REFUGE

TETON
N.F.

GROS VENTRE
WILDERNESS

Jackson

Driggs

Victor

IDAHO
WYOMING

Lavish landscape of sharp-cut mountains, shining lakes, and alpine meadows strewn with flowers, the park takes its name from three granite peaks, dubbed Les Trois Tétons *by French-speaking trappers. When established in 1929, the park protected only the major block of the Teton Range and six small lakes at the base of the mountains. In 1950 Congress extended the park to include part of the valley of Jackson Hole.*

as waterskiing, that seem more suitable to a national recreation area, park officials agree.

"If you were starting all over and could wipe the slate clean," said then Park Superintendent Jack Stark, "some of them probably wouldn't be permitted. If I could wave a magic wand I would change Jackson Lake back to its natural state."

All this in a park of 309,590 acres—less than a seventh the size of Yellowstone—and yet the contagion endures. I sensed it at daybreak from the outer park road when the rakish, cocked-hat peak of the Grand suddenly glowed pink, fired up by an unseen sun, while the valley of Jackson Hole slept in shadow. And in the evening with the sun hanging behind the somber mountains, when splayed fingers of light purpled the undersides of clouds. And on a stormy afternoon when lightning danced in the Tetons, a wild, random flash-dancing in a churning gray billow that turbaned the peaks and wove down the slopes, filling nearby canyons.

Southwest of Jenny Lake, in a tight cluster spanning four miles, spire the towers, massive and humbling, of what has been called the Cathedral Group: Teewinot Mountain, 12,325 feet; Mount Owen, 12,928; the Grand, 13,770; Middle Teton, 12,804; South Teton, 12,514; and 11,901-foot Nez Perce. The latter is also known as Howling Dog—viewed from the north its cleft peak resembles the open muzzle of a beast baying at the heavens.

West of Togwotee Pass spreads a wide-angle panorama, encompassing most of the stars of the 40-mile range, from Buck Mountain in the south, to the climactic Cathedral Group, northward to Rockchuck Peak and the stand-alone bulk of Mount Moran. "The first time I came over Togwotee I was eight," recalled Hank Phibbs, as we rested amid cathedral buttresses in Garnet Canyon. "I saw the Tetons and I thought, this must be close to heaven." Today he lives in Jackson and practices law there, a few miles south of the park; he attends the high places in all seasons, and, through service in the hierarchy of the Jackson Hole Alliance and the Greater Yellowstone Coalition, campaigns against defilement.

*T*he contagion of the Tetons makes Jackson Hole the home or the summer venue of scientists and diplomats, of people distinguished in the creative arts and people distinguished in creative exhaustion. Here you can also find waitpersons of culture and cosmopolitan tang, who may offer nuanced judgments not only on the local cuisine but also on the San Francisco restaurant scene, the ferment in Napa vineyards, the grand and bourgeois cru wines of the Haut Médoc, and the spiritual climate of Nepal—whither some are bound as soon as the budget permits. And you're doing the Grand? Oh, neat, they say.

The stifled yawn is forgivable. "Jackson," said Hank Phibbs, "has a lot of hard bodies, and they do fantastic things." A colleague of mine met one in a grocery checkout line. Of a chivalrous bent, he opened with a knight's gambit, a tale of arduous adventure. He told of backpacking along the Teton Crest Trail, behind the high peaks, camping in Alaska Basin amid the annual riot of wildflowers, and descending into Jackson Hole via Cascade Canyon—25, perhaps 30, withering miles in 2 1/2 days. The listener smiled in recognition. "Oh yes," she said, "I run that." Checkmate.

Jackson bodies harden themselves on the mountains

and on the streams, on foot and on skis, on horses and bicycles, in kayaks and canoes. One park ranger I know preaches a vigorous sermonette against the cult of "risk recreation" that worships speed and daredevilry and knows or cares little of Teton ecology or earth history.

He is spitting into a gale. Local publications display skiers forward flipping down a couloir, kayakers porpoising through torrents of froth, snowmobilers racing up slopes with most of their tread in the air. Beach boys bring their boards to surf the white water. Skiers come down the Grand. Of course, they have to climb it first; there are no lifts. Each year an unofficial race to be the first to reach the summit begins on New Year's Day. Some race against time; the swiftest can do it up the Grand and down in 12 hours in winter, a little over three hours in summer. A round-trip of some 14 miles, a steep trip of 7,000 vertical feet each way. For ordinary mortals summer alone provides sufficient challenge; even then the climb stretches over two days and may become, as Langford wrote, the severest labor of a lifetime.

Glacier-hewn canyons divide the Teton peaks and slice into the heart of the range. Through such corridors, wrote Fryxell, "the traveler mounts, step by step, to the spacious mountain halls of the high country." They are not merely conduits to the peak tops. For tens of thousands of visitors they are memorable destinations in themselves, tonic hikes. Occasionally I joined the summer hikers, poking into these steep-walled,

131

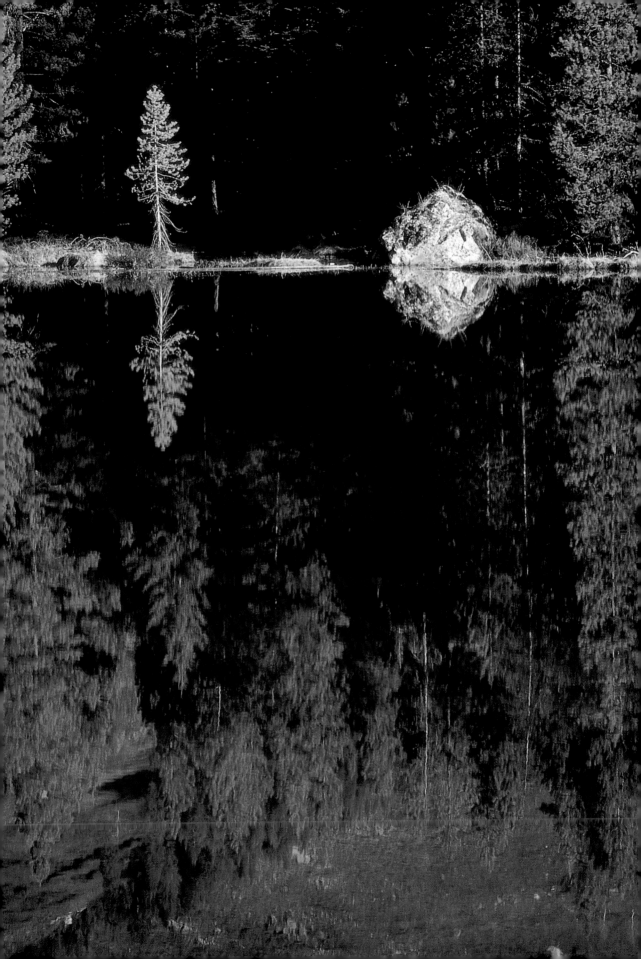

boulder-jumbled, creek-threaded chasms.

Cascade Canyon, most popular of all, offers a range of opportunities to day-hikers, from a tentative probe ending at a scenic vantage point, to a challenging trek up to a high amphitheater. Many hikers begin with a boat ride across Jenny Lake, one of the park gems impounded by moraines. A short walk above the boat landing leads to the cascades of Hidden Falls. A bit farther, Inspiration Point looks out across the lake and Jackson Hole to the Gros Ventre Range and the Mount Leidy highlands. With the Tetons lording it over the landscape, the modest highlands are not a breathtaking sight; yet Jackson environmentalists focus on them intently. The bald spots of clear-cut logging are easily seen and often lamented. There are oil leases pending in the highlands, and drilling permits have been issued.

Two miles westward into Cascade the canyon walls rise nearly a mile above the floor, to the crest line of the peaks. Beyond that the canyon walls get lower as the mountains—

Still waters reflect dense stands of lodgepole pine along the shores of String Lake (left), site of a popular picnic area. From another vantage point, the same lake mirrors a concentration of craggy peaks–part of the Teton Range–rising abruptly from the valley floor.

Teewinot to the south and Mount St. John to the north—slope down westward. One would expect the waters to crest here as well, flowing to the west from this point. But Cascade Creek continues to flow eastward, toward Jackson Hole. This is due to the much steeper east face of the Tetons. On the eastern incline, waters cut more powerfully, gnawing back into the mountains beyond the high points of the peaks. Thus the Teton Crest, the watershed of the range, lies well to the west of the peak tops.

A classic Cascade Canyon day hike ends at 9,035-foot-high

Lake Solitude, nestling in a rock-walled cirque that rises another thousand feet. I picnicked there rather hurriedly one afternoon, eager to return in time to catch the last boat. If I missed it, the seven miles back would increase by two miles of Jenny Lake perimeter. But when I headed back down the north end of Cascade Creek, the V of the canyon cupped the summits of the Grand, Owen, and Teewinot. As the descent progressed the angles shifted, the mighty triad loomed closer, scarves of cloud swirled about them. I had not come to hurry from that.

Another day I made for the mouth of Death Canyon, where lies the most ancient rock of the Tetons, gneissic layers more than 2.87 billion years old. Thunder ricocheted as I approached, and a dark cloud filled the wedge of sky. I turned instead to the trail around Phelps Lake to enjoy the unclouded vistas of Jackson Hole. Laurance S. Rockefeller's J-Y Ranch rims the lake's southern edge, but the ranch buildings seem well hidden from the park trail. I saw no sign of them.

The J-Y was the first dude ranch in the valley, with a choice view of the Teton landscape. Originally, the holding spread across some 3,300 acres. Most of the ranch is now owned by the park, after a series of land deals in which Rockefeller gave two-thirds of the acreage to charities. As for the remaining acres, Rockefeller and the park have negotiated a scenic easement that prevents any additional development. According to George Lamb, a Rockefeller associate, the value of the easement, appraised at 5.6 million dollars, has been donated to the Memorial Sloan-Kettering Cancer Center.

One day I wandered a short way up the Granite Canyon Trail, but got waylaid by a fine grove of aspens, wildflowers in the understory, tiny birds clenching bugs in their bills, buzzing around nest holes. Yellowstone country dotes on "quaky" aspen. There is not that much of it; what there is has not been thriving. About half of Yellowstone Park's aspen trees have been lost or have gone to shrub. Critics of park management say the swelling elk herds nibble the young aspen shoots to death. Elk do browse aspen; however other factors may be at work, too. While park biologists consider years of drought and fire supression may have a role, no clear-cut answers are at hand. An aspect of research following the 1988 fires has shown that fire may not play a significant role in aspen recovery. Even after years of research there are still more questions than answers.

Aspens are famous for autumn gold; their summer tone in Granite Canyon was more subdued, but still bright and airy, with shimmering leaves and silvery green trunks, with a sort of lime interior light, in soft focus. I wondered what an Impressionist painter would make of the scene.

Of the lakes that are strung along the canyon mouths, six put together could fit into the seventh, 17-mile-long Jackson Lake. A dam completed in 1916 raised the lake level 39 feet and left a notorious mess of floating trees and debris. "Liver Pill signs on the Statue of Liberty wouldn't be half as bad as this," moaned a visiting United States senator. That mess was long gone when, in the mid-1980s, Jackson Lake suffered an aesthetic relapse—a huge swath of drab bed exposed as the lake was drawn down for dam reconstruction. The ordeal was reinforced, betimes, by the chuffing and clanking of a 32-ton weight dropping to compact earth for the dam, part of the 82-million-dollar renovation project.

The Snake River flows out of the lake here and soon weaves through the Oxbow Bend. Götterdämmerung reconstruction did not diminish the pleasures of an evening on the oxbow. I paddled the meandering waters with Carl Schreier, writer, artist, photographer, naturalist, and slave of Yellowstone country. There were pelicans afloat, cormorants diving, mergansers everywhere, a gadwall putting distance between herself and four or five ducklings as we paddled by. There were sandhill cranes honking out of sight, and one soaring above on translucent wings. By the shore a bull moose came up with a snoutful of dripping vegetation—"moose muck," said Carl. Diving beavers made the biggest splash, flapping down in noisy bursts; no 9.8 divers in that tribe. We ran out of daylight and oxbow simultaneously. Perfect timing.

Garnet Canyon is one of the busiest hubs of Teton mountaineering, funneling climbers to South Teton, Nez Perce, Cloudveil Dome, Middle Teton, and the most popular routes to the Grand. My companions and I began our ascent of the Grand, as thousands do each year, in Lupine Meadows at 6,760 feet. We chose late August, a good bet for fine climbing weather—though the Tetons make no promises. Jackson Hole had acquired its late-summer tan, hinting at autumn, when we left the Lupine flat, crossed a wooded moraine and switchbacked up into watered meadows and talus slopes, slanting glaciers and towering rock walls.

We were a loosely strung group that included Hank Phibbs and Rick Reese, author of Greater Yellowstone, a pioneering compendium of what to guard in the ecosystem—and what to guard against. Rick and another of our group, Mike Ermarth, were old climbing mates, members of the honored team that in 1967 safely extracted a fallen climber—he had multiple compound leg fractures—from 13,000 feet on the harsh north face of the Grand.

That north face, looming above Teton Glacier, was hidden from us in Garnet Canyon. We hiked the south side, the least harsh side, the turnpike route to the Grand Teton summit, so to speak. Rick, Mike, and Hank had come for recreation. Al Read, Raymond Gehman, and I were on business, Al guiding, Raymond and I laboring. In the '60s Al held an appointment in the Foreign Service. Assigned from Nepal to Washington, D.C., he resigned and turned to professional mountaineering. Veteran climbers hold him in high regard, a man who has known Himalayan heights. Still a diplomat, withal, he patiently monitors novices' slow-motion exertions.

Up ahead, there appears to be respite for the weary, a stairway to a summit or an elevator, perhaps, in the black band

FOLLOWING PAGES: *Sunrise on the Teton Crest Trail illuminates the stark flanks of Mount Meek and casts long shadows at a backpacker's campsite. Overnight treks into the backcountry require a permit from the National Park Service, which also operates five campgrounds. Moose and Colter Bay visitor centers offer information on a variety of ranger-led activities— short hikes, boat rides, children's events, and campfire programs.*

running up the middle of the Middle Teton. "People all the time ask if that's a man-made structure," said Al, "and when I tell them it's a natural feature they're sort of appalled." This is one of the famous black dikes of the Tetons, formed over a billion years ago when magma flowed into fissures and solidified. And when the young range began to rise along its fault system some nine million years ago and erosion gradually scoured away the sedimentary overburden, the black dikes stood out on the gray-brown, gneissic flanks.

Below the dike ahead of us lie features that produced another illusion. In 1925 a climbing party, out to explore the tallest Teton, toiled up what appeared from below to be the eastern slopes of the Grand. On reaching the summit they found, to their disappointment, a huge gap between them and Grand Teton. We were not tempted by the buttresses of Disappointment Peak as we mounted the canyon.

We paused near the Platforms, a flat area named for the tent platforms of the Civilian Conservation Corps, which built the canyon trails in the 1930s. "The area is under rehabilitation, as you can see from the signs," said Al. "There used to be a little grassy area, our favorite lunch spot. All the grass, flowers, everything, have been tramped down. So they rerouted the trail through the talus and moraine, and so long as people stay on the rocks, the area can eventually recover."

Our long day ended on the Lower Saddle, a bouldery ridge 11,600 feet high, curving between the Middle and the Grand. From the west, where the Idaho plains faded into the dusk, wind bellowed up, rattling the guide hut, a big hollow bread loaf of plastic. Backpacks were emptied. On went pile suits and shell parkas, gloves and wool hats; in went hot tea and soup, noodles and cookies. Some of us laid claim to the lee side of boulders and hunched down there.

Middle Teton, despite its patchy coating of ice and snow, looked user-friendly, but we would be heading the other way. The Grand looked . . . well, as the man said, it's there. We were not alone. The big hut filled with a dozen or so teenagers. They played cards, read comic books; the talk, in current fashion, veered from silly to salty, all exhibition, no inhibition. If the pitted crag staring down from the north end of the saddle stirred any awe in them, it did not surface. They had been together for six weeks of wilderness adventure. Here it would end. In look and manner they appeared fit and rosy, pumped up for the morrow, and undaunted.

*D*istanced from them by a generation and more, I felt closer to Pip's old schoolmarm in Great Expectations, a "woman of limited means and unlimited infirmity, who used to go to sleep from six to seven every evening, in the society of youth"—sleep, in this case, bedeviled by writhing and snoring, three of us in a small tent, elbow to backbone. Nature, without mercy, deploys all manner of urging to extract a body from its down sheath. Stay, says the sleeping bag; listen to the wind out there; savor the warmth in here. Such is the pillow talk of claustrophilia.

The youngsters awoke with unabated liveliness, abating the predawn grimness—the low clouds, the spectral Tetons on either hand, the ceaseless wind. Before long, another boost to morale: Far to the east, above the Wind River Range, gold streaked the sky. Twenty-one hundred feet to go.

It began with a steep hike along the line of the saddle, a grunt, as they say in these parts. Up we went, across the black dike that bands the Grand, past the tower called the Needle, beside a couloir hollowed by glaciation and expanded by rockfall. If this route is followed all the way—and if the weather holds and the rock is dry—it is one of the simpler climbs to the top. It is the Owen-Spalding route, named for the leaders of the historic 1898 climb. William Owen failed several times; when he succeeded in 1898, he campaigned long and hard to deny Langford the primacy. Owen's partner, Franklin Spalding, a more generous spirit, placed far less importance on competition. "Whether I was first or thousandth," he wrote Langford, "the climb was worthwhile." Owen finally won official—but not unanimous—recognition

Wilderness garden: Radiant summer blooms crowd a high mountain meadow on the Teton Crest Trail. Clusters of leaflike bracts give the rhexia-leaved paintbrush its scarlet color. Yellow groundsels reach toward purple lupines. Pink mountain townsendia (below) brighten a rocky outcrop. Hardy alpine and subalpine plants growing in Teton highlands have adapted to weather extremes and high winds.

"in the open meadows unnumbered flowers spring to life and beauty"

–Fritiof Fryxell
The Tetons: Interpretations of a Mountain Landscape, 1938

*E*ars cocked, a mule deer pauses in a clearing in Cascade Canyon. Named

for its big ears, the deer shares its range with moose and elk, browsing grasses and woody plants. 143

for his team as the first to ascend the summit.

Time for our team to rope up, to begin the belaying. Belay. The word rings across the years. How many Navy chiefs have I heard barking: "Belay that!" to countermand an order or stop some tomfoolery. Sailing men secure, or belay, lines. Mountaineers belay each other up difficult pitches. Teams of two or more climbers are tied in to one rope. The belayer anchors to a rock or tree, or, as here, braces against a ledge or rock, then passes the rope around his or her body and keeps it taut as the climber ascends.

The first belay on the Grand did not go well. I fumbled the figure eight tie-in knot, then let the rope fall loose as Raymond Gehman mounted instead of drawing it up without slack. Forced to conduct remedial knot-tying and belaying at 12,000 feet, Al displayed a bit of the tartness of an old Navy chief: "This is no time to be learning the belay," he said. "You have to do it right." Day before yesterday was climbing school, beside Hidden Falls above Jenny Lake, and everybody passed. Today, Gehman is at the end of the line, young and durable, but not unbreakable. Aye-aye, sir. Though matters improved rapidly, Raymond's skepticism remained unbounded. Thenceforth, at the merest hint of a slackening, his fine alpine tenor rang out against the rock: "Up rope!"

Beyond the rock tunnel called the Eye of the Needle and around the corner known as the Belly-Roll Almost, our path diverged from Owen-Spalding to a more difficult and more interesting route. How it was discovered is one of the great stories of Jackson Hole, often told, celebrated in film documentaries. I heard it in a roundabout way, partly from Al Read, partly from the discoverer, with tangent threads from various sources.

After Owen-Spalding, no one ascended the summit of the Grand until 1923, a passage of 25 years. For the valley folk, as Paul Petzoldt has written, climbing made no sense "if you ain't lost nothing up there." Petzoldt arrived in Jackson in 1924, eventually to become the first Teton climbing guide. In the '20s, today's Grand Teton Park was mostly national forest and ranchland. Development threatened the valley, and local leaders, including dude and cattle ranchers, proposed federal protection for a "museum on the hoof," where tourists could enjoy an unspoiled landscape and where dudes might get a taste of ways of the Old West.

In 1926 John D. Rockefeller, Jr., journeyed south from Yellowstone, accompanied by Horace Albright. A self-guiding trail on Lunch Tree Hill, beside Jackson Lake Lodge, marks the picnic stop where Rockefeller caught the Teton contagion. "The impressive mountain vistas . . . inspired Mr. Rockefeller," reads a sign, "but later he was appalled by the increasing number of tawdry commercial enterprises found further south. Jenny Lake sported a dance hall at the time." (The day I read these forebodings of the 1920s, a country-and-western trio held forth in the Stockade Bar at the nearby lodge.)

Working with Albright, Rockefeller undertook to buy up land, got caught in the decades of bitter dispute over the future of Jackson Hole, and eventually made a major contribution to the shape of Grand Teton National Park, with a donation of more than 30,000 acres. The John D. Rockefeller, Jr., Memorial Parkway was named in his honor; his son Laurance continues the family interest in parkland conservation.

As for the dance hall at Jenny Lake—not tawdry at all, says a man who played saxophone and clarinet in the band. "It was very well run," he recalls. "There were some pretty wild dances—that's the way all dances were then."

The musician, just starting college, was a protégé of Paul Petzoldt. One day in 1931, as they came up the Owen-Spalding route with two Austrian clients, Petzoldt suggested that the teenager explore a ridge to the east, which might provide an alternate summit route. The approach to the ridge is along a ledge that Petzoldt dubbed Wall Street for the tremendous rock walls above and below it; the other Wall Street was much in mind in those Depression days. The youngster headed up Wall Street. Now in retirement in Moose, Wyoming, he recalls the day without hesitation: "It was my second time on the mountain. I was wearing Paul's football shoes, with leather cleats, about a size 11. I had several pairs of socks on, but I still felt like I was on roller skates."

Wall Street starts out comfortably wide, but after more than a hundred yards the ledge narrows to nothing. "Paul said to call if I didn't like the way it looked," he continued. "It scared me to death. I came back and called but the wind was against me. So I thought I would take another look. It looked worse. I screamed then. I did that seven times." Each time he screamed, and each time his courage returned,

Ending a grueling half-day climb, Sy Fishbein and photographer Raymond Gehman claim the rocky summit of the Grand Teton. Even the easiest routes to the top require rock-climbing skills and roping-up for safety. Taking the express way down, the author (left) rappels off an overhang. He slides the rope through his right hand to control the speed of his descent.

FOLLOWING PAGES: Lofty ramparts of the Teton Range bestow a special grandeur on Jackson Hole, a valley realm gleaming with the autumn gold of aspen. No foothills soften the mountain range's sheer rise.

leading to still another look. After the seventh trip he noticed some projecting flakes above where the ledge all but petered out. He thought if he could use those to climb up and out as high as it was possible to go, then there would be only a leap of about eight to ten feet across and down to a boulder. And that is what he did, in outsize football cleats, all alone, no rope, and 1,500 feet of nothing below.

Once on the ridge, he found a route to the summit, as Petzoldt had predicted, and was sitting there when his mentor and the Austrians arrived an hour and a half later. Then he wasted no time getting down. "Had to get ready for a dance," he told me. "Played till one o'clock in the morning." He went on to a career of music and mountaineering, climbing in the Tetons in summer, supervising music education in Idaho during the school year. He is Glenn Exum. The ridge he scouted is the Exum Ridge, and a guide service in Jackson Hole bears his name. Al Read is part owner of it.

Today the route from the disappearing ledge of Wall Street involves no ten-foot jump, needless to say. The course is horizontal; climbers use Glenn's footholds as handholds, in a snug belay, wearing boots that fit—and grip the rock. This pitch ends with a step to a foothold, a lean to a handhold, and a climb up to the famous boulder. Understandably, Wall Street is a much duller story now. One way to make it more exciting is to look down and start counting those 1,500 feet, perhaps while stepping up to the boulder.

Among the scores of present-day routes to the Grand Teton summit, Exum's ranks as the most popular by far—"probably," wrote Orrin and Lorraine Bonney in their Guide to the Wyoming Mountains and Wilderness Areas, "because it is the guides' favorite. It has about 1,500 feet of enjoyable climbing compared to the last 600 feet of the Spalding-Owen route." Another reason for the popularity of the Exum Ridge appears just above Wall Street. It is the 60-foot pitch of the Golden Staircase, golden rock and, weather permitting, a golden morning. The route is on the sunny side from there on up, and the view lengthens out to encompass Jackson Hole. This must be, for the veterans, the best stretch; most of the enjoyable climbing occurs in these upper heights, including the so-called Friction Pitch.

The name denotes a steep rock surface without a protrusion or crack to step on or cling to, where only the friction of hands and boot soles against the rock, along with proper body position, holds the weight. Flies know the problem.

By today's standards a friction pitch is "billiard-ball smooth," said Rick Reese. The one on Exum Ridge won the name in the Model-T era of mountaineering and these days is worthy of it only when glazed with ice. It's rather dished out, observed Rick, with concavities that can be used for holds. Al Read concurred. As leader, up he went, with no one to belay him on the 130-foot pitch.

So the holds must be there, but where? The worst came first, some 20 feet of it, up and out to the right. There was unevenness in the rock, to be sure, but nothing I would stake my weight on. I spent an awful lot of time dawdling, scanning, testing. A hand slipped a bit here, a foot glitched there. Back to square one. There was no friction out there, only in the belly. A forbidden thought—a pull on the rope, maybe, to help get a purchase? Nope; the rope is for emergencies, the last resort, not the first. Finally, a hand gripped, a boot held, even as the creaking torso levered up. So it went, incredibly, until, beyond the 20 feet some credible knobs and hollows began to show up. After much too long a while, I could see Al Read at the top of the pitch, holding a taut rope, calmly observing my snail's pace.

The morning—sometimes golden, mostly gray— ended, the belays ended, the rope was coiled. It was simply a scramble, edging around a snowfield, clambering up boulders, finally to sit on one of them. It was time to smile and stare, at the neighboring Cathedrals, at Jackson Hole, at the Idaho plains. And above, where, at last, there was only sky. The spirit of vanity fair creeps in—a little self-preening, the mind shaping images of pluck and fortitude for home consumption. Then I looked over at Al Read, popping lemon drops, gazing into the distance, and I remembered having asked him how often the guides came up the mountain. Oh, about once a week, he replied. The images faded. Better to concentrate on reality.

Cascade Creek was a scratch, Lake Solitude a puddle. Disappointment Peak loomed just below us in one direction; in another the Grand slopes 500 feet down to the Upper Saddle, whose far end rises to the West Spur. There lie the jumbled remains of a man-made stone structure named the Enclosure. No one knows who built it, but it is a testament, evidence that prehistoric climbers reached 13,280 feet, at least. If they turned back at the West Spur, no surprise. Many in historic times have done so; from that point the steep, icy west face of the Grand bears a frightening aspect.

Jackson Hole looked table-flat. Distance or weary eyes—or both—smoothed out the buttes and dips. From down there the peak looks sharp and clean cut, solid. I had often wondered what it was really like. Now I know. The peak is really a heap of chiseled rock and scattered boulders. Wind, snow, thaw, freeze—and time—are relentless; the crown of the Grand is slowly cracking up.

When it was first established in 1929, Grand Teton National Park contained little more than mountains. During the struggles over expansion, some felt the sagebrush sprawl of Jackson Hole didn't quite belong—too commonplace. Reading the history, I learned that Olaus Murie, wildlife biologist and wilderness rover, beheld the valley and the heights as a unity, both essential to the park. He believed also that the pleasures of the natural world intensify along with the effort it takes to seek them out.

Olaus was right.

FOLLOWING PAGES: Tour bus passengers watch cowboys working cattle at one of the grazing areas in the park. Ranchers who had grazing permits on lands incorporated into the park in 1950 retained those rights. Since 1950, the National Park Service has pursued an active land acquisition program, purchasing inholdings within the park. As of 1996, one cattle ranch and a dude ranch remain privately owned.

GREATER

YELLOWSTONE

Autumn into Winter

*T*he bison have rutted, the elk are bugling, and the aspens gleam as summer yields to autumn. The music and the color—Grand Teton Superintendent Jack Stark believed the season's turning lifts his mountain park to a peak of beauty. The sight and sound of elk lure hikers to the meadows along Cottonwood Creek, around Bradley and Taggart and Jenny Lakes, out on the RKO ranch road, whose name recalls the days when Hollywood cowboys fought range wars in Jackson Hole. Early and late in the day are best, when elk venture from forest cover to graze nearby meadows. In Yellowstone late-season campers at Mammoth Hot Springs and Madison may enjoy a little night music of bugling bulls.

With deepening cold and snow in the high summer range, elk filter down through forest and meadow. Poachers stalk the parkland edges—and so do the rangers. "Some people," said the veteran Jerry Mernin, of Yellowstone's Snake River district, "like to hunt both sides of the boundary." At times outfitters scout the migration routes for trophy bulls, choice game for clients who pay $2,000 and more for a ten-day hunt from tent camps in breathtaking national forest backcountry.

Not all hunters are dreaming of an imperial bull—a rare one with seven-point antlers. An old forest ranger I know, more interested in putting meat on the table than in hanging heads on his walls, prefers to hunt cows or spike bulls (young ones with unbranched antlers). The big bulls are gamy, he says, carrying with them the odors of the rut.

Guiding hunters is an important business in this storied big-game country, and outfitters have a stake in a healthy ecosystem. At times they make common cause with environmentalists, steadfastly opposing large-scale logging. "Nobody wants to camp on tree stumps," said a Wyoming outfitter operating in a valley targeted for timber sales. In places the high-country camps themselves, with scores of horses and huge caches of feed, have a troublesome impact.

"Some of those sites," said biologist Al Boss of the Bridger-Teton National Forest, "look like they've been hammered into the ground." He was talking about camps in designated national forest wilderness—where, in the grand vision of the Wilderness Act of 1964, "the earth and its community of life are untrammeled by man."

Through the seasons I returned again and again to explore the far reaches and the issues of Yellowstone country. I drove the back roads, visited mines and mills and refuges, rode and hiked the wilderness trails and, finally, skied the frozen, steaming, pinch-yourself heart of it.

Summer's end in 1987 marked the beginning of the end for an Amoco wildcat rig that rose the equivalent of some 17 stories at the eastern edge of the spectacular Beartooth Highway, near Red Lodge, Montana. The site was on private land next to a Custer National Forest slope so steep that Amoco had to drill in from the side.

A friend of mine, traveling the tight spaghetti bends of the Beartooth Highway over the granite plateaus, past the

"where happiness and contentment seemed to reign in wild romantic splendor"

–Osborne Russell
1835 in *Journal of a Trapper*

Summer on the wane, Erin Gorsuch and her poodle share Yellowstone's autumn carnival of sights, sounds, and scents. Color bursts out high in the mountains and works its way down to the foothills. The high-pitched bugling of bull elk echoes through the mountains.

Shimmering gold field: In autumn a sweep of aspens (below) curves southward along Jackson Hole to the distant Gros Ventre Range. Beyond evergreens and aspens (right), grassland slopes north to Yellow-stone's Buffalo Plateau.

FOLLOWING PAGES: Flaming shrubs and a slender aspen glow against a canvas of lodgepole pine and spruce.

krummholz with its gnarled trees, the chilly lakes, and the alpine rock gardens with their tiny tundra flowers, spotted the roadside wildcat tower when he reached the valley floor. "It was like a slap in the face," he said. Other tourists, however, were intrigued. What's going on? How does it work? asked the Rocky Mountain subspecies of sidewalk superintendent. By April 1988 Amoco had pierced down through more than 15,800 feet of rock—nearly three miles. Nothing. The company abandoned the site. Eleven million dollars down a dry hole.

Environmentalists ask, "What if . . . ?" What if the wildcat had struck oil? A grove of producing wells, a tank farm, truck traffic, at a gateway to one of the most scenic highways in the nation? But energy workers squeezed by years of bust ask, "Why not?" More than four million acres of Yellowstone country are under lease or have lease applications pending for oil and gas exploration.

Chevron and its partner in the Stillwater Mining Company had more success in the Beartooths than Amoco. In the rugged north face of the range, at the edge of the ecosystem, Stillwater is tapping one of the richest bonanzas of platinum and related minerals outside the Soviet Union, South Africa, and

Canada. Until Stillwater's mine began producing ore in 1987, the United States imported nearly every ounce of these costly and rare metals—used in chemicals and electronics, in heart pacemakers and anticancer drugs, in lead-free gas and the catalytic converters that remove pollutants from car exhaust. In the big picture, prized platinum jewelry is small potatoes—less than 2 percent of U.S. use.

By late summer of 1988 Stillwater was mining 700 tons

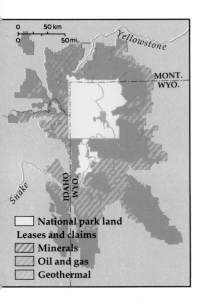

Multiple uses of Yellowstone country: Official surveys show logging areas (map, below) and those promising minerals and energy (map, above). Fears for the geysers gave rise to a law restricting geothermal drilling nearby. Poisonous legacies linger at such sites as the arsenic plant of the old Jardine gold mine (opposite) at Yellowstone's northern edge. A new gold venture there promises no toxic outflows and plans to eliminate or contain sources of the arsenic.

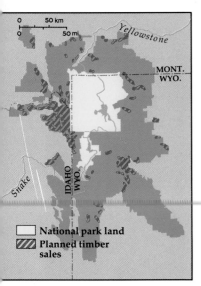

of ore a day out of a thin, steeply slanting layer of ancient crystallized magma 28 miles long. Two quarterly reports on file with the Montana Department of Revenue showed a total yield of 32,343.7 ounces of platinum, sold for about $500 an ounce, and 111,196.2 ounces of palladium, at about $122 an ounce. The six-month gross totaled nearly 30 million dollars.

Gross numbers do not tell the whole story, noted then mine manager Joe Dewey. Stillwater had plowed 84 million dollars into the operation and saw no bottom line in the black for 14 months after the mine opened. Dewey insisted the mine would do no harm to its surroundings. No mine water would discharge into streams, and more than half of the solid tailings would go back into the excavations.

Phil Jaquith was district ranger of the Custer National Forest's Beartooth region, which includes the Amoco site as well as the Stillwater mine—and most of the peaks in Montana that rise above 12,000 feet. For a mine of its size, observed Jaquith as we toured the complex, the Stillwater operation has a minimal environmental impact. "It's such a beautiful area," he added, "it's too bad the minerals were laid down in this location."

Each year some 15,000 forest visitors pass by the mine as they head up Stillwater Canyon into the Absaroka-Beartooth Wilderness, which lies partly in the Gallatin Forest. Stillwater's Woodbine Campground is at one of the busiest trailheads in the Absaroka-Beartooth—the country's fifth most popular wilderness. With that ranking, it's no surprise that the Absaroka-Beartooth has at times come under pressure. "We're the outdoor bedroom of Billings," said Jaquith. It is there, in the largest population center of Montana, that the Custer district sends missionaries to preach the gospel of "no-trace camping." The message is aimed at schoolchildren, many of whom are past and future wilderness users. The classroom programs have won praise from environmentalists.

A few years ago wilderness ranger Blase Di Lulo came up with one of his many ideas to relieve pressure on overused campgrounds. Along the popular trails of his East Rosebud area, Di Lulo gathered horse manure and spread it over battered campsites. Campers found other sites, while the topping provided rest and nutrient to tired, trampled ground.

West of Custer, beyond Yellowstone Park, summer's end marks another season of reckoning in the long effort to succor two of the historic players in the ecosystem: the trumpeter swan, largest waterfowl in the world, and the critically endangered whooping crane, America's tallest bird.

Greater Yellowstone, with its thermal waters and mountain-girt remoteness, provided the last haven for the trumpeter in the lower 48 states. In 1988, nearly all of Canada's breeding population of trumpeters, some 1,800 strong, found winter refuge here; now some 2,700 birds migrate here. In addition some 380, known as the Tristate Subpopulation, reside year-round. To the casual eye all goes swimmingly with them. In Yellowstone Park I saw trumpeters nesting at Beach Springs and cygnets swimming with parents on the Madison

River. On Flat Creek in Jackson Hole I saw one in repose, motionless on a frozen ledge, like a centerpiece of ice sculpture on a banquet table.

In Red Rock Lakes National Wildlife Refuge, under the brow of the Centennial Mountains, I saw a hen heaped on her nest mound, incubating eggs, while the cob took a stately cruise around their pond, crossing paths with a brace of pintail drakes. Red Rock Lakes was established half a century ago to protect the last known survivors of the species. The flock built up, leveled off, and then, while the Canadian migrants continued to increase, the year-round trumpeter population fell into a puzzling decline. In the 1980s some years produced a total of only four fledglings. An in-depth study by biologist Ruth Shea pointed to the underlying problem—the birds' loss of their migratory instincts. With the flocks congregating in winter in a habitat unable to support them all, the difficulties of finding adequate nesting conditions and food supplies were magnified.

In 1987, after a heavy outpouring of winter grain, better control of water levels, and favorable nesting weather, summer's end found 96 trumpeter fledglings—more than twice the number of any earlier year in the decade.

Between 1988 and 1996 the Tristate population declined dramatically. What Ruth Shea feared might happen did: About 100 birds died following a February snow storm in 1989 and likely more birds, weakened by the harsh winter died on their migration north. As Ruth says, "The trumpeters of Red Rocks were like the grizzlies of Yellowstone in the 1970s when they were accustomed to feeding on garbage rather than foraging for themselves." Then, during the winter of 1989 and 1990 a record number of waterfowl overwintered, and there was a die-off of aquatic plants. The combination was a near catastrophe. "That was the straw that broke the camel's back," Ruth says. A secure recovery requires the establishment of new wintering grounds and that trumpeters relearn some of the migratory traditions their ancestors knew. As with the grizzlies of Yellowstone, feeding was stopped. Birds were discouraged from wintering by lowering pond levels, causing disturbances, and pairs were trapped and moved to favorable habitats at Grays Lake and in southern Oregon. After six years, a new generation of trumpeters bypasses Red Rocks and Harriman State Park to migrate farther south in Idaho and into Utah. There is a separate population of almost ten thousand trumpeters in Alaska; before Europeans arrived the swans trumpeted across the continent, coast to coast.

The shrill whoops of whooping cranes sounded across the land from eastern grasslands to the Rockies. Once they dwelt in the Bechler Meadows of Yellowstone. Now only one summers in the Bechler's marshes, ideal habitat. It is from the foster hatch of sandhill cranes nesting in the bulrushes and cattails of Grays Lake National Wildlife Refuge, in southeastern Idaho. Here

164   *Elk recline on the grounds of Mammoth Hot Springs, site of historic*

Fort Yellowstone, park headquarters since the United States Army built it in 1891.

biologist Rod Drewien nursed the hope of planting a new nesting population of a species that numbered only about 30 breeding pairs in the wild.

Until 1988 Rod received a dozen or two fertilized whooper eggs from the only known nesting ground, in Canada, and placed them in sandhill nests at Grays Lake. In 14 years the surrogate parents hatched 100; about 20 survived. At summer's end they departed with the sandhills, and so did Drewien. "I chased them up and down the country," he says. To the San Luis Valley of Colorado, south to the Rio Grande marshes of New Mexico, and, in spring, back north. So far only male whoopers return to Grays Lake; by late April, with hormone levels peaking, they are whooping it up for mates. In vain. The only female hangs out in Greater Yellowstone, mainly in the Bechler backcountry and other marshes, wingloose and fancy-free. Who knows why?

For a decade Rod Drewien played a passive role, just watching and hoping. Then he launched a more aggressive matchmaking strategy. Deep in the night, in hip boots, with an aircraft landing light on a football helmet, with a power source strapped to his back, and wielding a long-handled net, he stalked the females in the shallows where they roosted.

He caught a few and brought them to Grays Lake. But it was late in the season; male ardor had cooled. One fall a few temporarily paired off—and the pairs actually migrated together. "I mean we stood there and watched them leaving, several sets of twos," Rod recalled. "Things looked great. We were elated." He sounded like a bubbling parent whose spinster daughters had just acquired steadies. But somewhere on migration, the pairs broke up. Fortunate that Rod is blessed with patience and good cheer. Playing Cupid in Yellowstone country, he needs a deep reservoir of both.

Fall's approach brings bands of domestic sheep down

from the high ridges, where they have been grazing, at bargain rates, on national forest land. Sometimes they graze in designated wilderness, as the law permits, sometimes in Situation 1 terrain, which means it is habitat whose highest priority is for grizzly bear use. In late summer of 1987, a band of a thousand sheep on Carrot Ridge in the Teton Range came down prematurely. A grizzly sow, with two cubs, had gotten into the band and feasted. The sheep were moved, but the sow followed and killed more of them. Years ago marauding grizzlies were slaughtered. Times have changed. Carrot Ridge lies on the west slope of the Teton Crest, in Targhee National Forest, in Jedediah Smith Wilderness, in Situation 1 habitat. Under the rules, the sheep had to leave the west slope.

Bruce Fox, the Targhee's district ranger there, arranged the move with the sheep owners, then set out, with me and about ten others, for a horse-camping trip, right up in that country coincidentally. We were crossing the crest from Grand Teton Park into the Targhee, via windblown Jackass Pass, when the belt radios started crackling. Through the static of a fierce little mountain squall, Bruce was summoned back to his office. Something about the sheep.

He was gone for most of next day, rejoining us at camp in Hidden Corral, a meadow cul-de-sac watered by South Bitch Creek (from *biche*, they say, French for "doe"). One of the sheep owners, Bruce reported, had gone off to a meeting of woolgrowers, where he told of having to remove his bloodied band for the convenience of a grizzly. Visiting dignitaries, including a deputy secretary of agriculture, began asking questions. Bruce explained the rules; little more was said. At camp he put away a steak, saddled his horse, and headed into the night, to help get the sheep off Carrot Ridge.

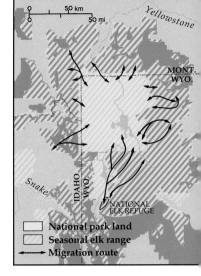

	National park land
	Seasonal elk range
➤	Migration route

*W*e left Hidden Corral and rode up over Dead Horse Pass (no need to ask how that got its name; just listen to the animals strain and pant) and down into the basin at Green Lake. During a breather there I talked with John Burns, supervisor of the Targhee, about environmental concerns clashing with historical uses of the forest, such as logging and grazing. Yes, John agreed, "there's an established local culture accustomed to using the land in a certain way, and if you push too hard against it you risk losing everything you're working for.

"Folks around here don't raise animals to be killed by other animals. It's almost biblical. You're responsible for your animals. A man feels that if he can't protect his animals he doesn't deserve to have them."

The grizzly sow came around again in 1988, and again the sheep departed. By all accounts, the days of sheep grazing on Carrot Ridge are numbered.

My horse in the Targhee, borrowed from the national forest stock, was well named; Ebony had the hue and sheen of an eight ball. Ebony was also well bred; a Missouri fox-trotter,

"autumn in Jackson Hole ...these perfect blue-and-gold days"

—Olaus Murie
Wapiti Wilderness, 1966

Facing a new future, a seven-month-old bighorn lamb, part of a program to reintroduce the sheep to former range, rests in the arms of John Talbott of the Wyoming Game and Fish Department at Whiskey Basin. Capturing the sheep calls for careful and concerted teamwork. Workers spread hay and apple pulp across the snow. For two weeks sheep gather to feast, enticed by the scent. Then workers hoist a net and drop it over the animals (opposite). Firm yet gentle wrestling brings the bighorns under control. Then weighing, ear tagging, and inoculations precede the trip to their new home; this 1987 operation reintroduced 47 bighorns to the Wind River Indian Reservation.

he moved with a cushiony side-to-side rhythm that meant balm to his spavined rider. The gait presumably resembles the short steps of a fox, steps that are also part of the dance I danced when the century and I were still young. Ebony and I fox-trotted comfortably, except when he fell out of step, into a regular trot. Then, from knees to torso, with parts in between, I felt once again the pounding I had known when a dude-wise quarter horse jigged me unmercifully in a distant corner of the ecosystem.

On both occasions I had been invited on an "orientation ride," where workers and managers of the parks and forests caravan into the backcountry for a few days. Weighty affairs of the ecosystem may make the agenda, but mostly it is the rightness of being out there—the feel of the wind and pelting rain, laboring across the divides, meadow and creek music and sundown, cowboy blues and campfire tales of hunting and wrangling, the way it was and, save for these vestigial days, will never be again. Days away from the office humdrum, the computers, internal combustion.

Oh yes, the food. Horse campers are not backpackers. They do not sit around debating the ultimate gorp mix, candied papaya versus yogurt-coated raisins; or fooling with little mixes that turn into fettuccine Alfredo. Rather they are into roast turkey and T-bone, Teton-size mounds of fried potatoes, ears of corn by the dozen. (Save the husks for the pack mules, fellas.) Pack strings can haul the heavy grub, and riding horses, of course, extends the range. But it takes hours of work, packing and unpacking heavy panniers and hoisting them beyond grizzly bear reach for the night; feeding the animals and hobbling them—and giving chase when the unhobbled run off. All this sandwiched around a day in the saddle over Rocky Mountain terrain. On balance, I will remain a gorp man.

On one such pack trip, over in Bridger-Teton National Forest, we rode the ridges of the Teton Wilderness, just south of Yellowstone. It would become scorched land in the blazing summer of '88, but this day it sparkled with mariposa lilies and lupine in bloom. Returning to camp one day we ran into the pack mules galloping up the trail, out of tether, heading cross-country. Not far behind them rode Grand Teton Park's Harold Dugan, creative linguist, behavioral psychologist, and mule skinner, practicing all his skills at once. Rounding up the mules, he fixed each with a stare and broadcast its scandalous pedigree, loud and clear. "Yeah," Harold replied defiantly to questioning glances, "I call them a lot of names—and they deserve most of them."

We camped at Fox Park, a meadow cradling headwaters of the Snake River. Most pitched tents well away from the dining area; but Ernie Nunn, then deputy supervisor of Bridger-Teton, spread his bedroll in the open, at the edge of the dining tarp. A few others gathered around to wish him sweet dreams. They wondered about the dinner smells wafting through the wilderness. Perhaps into the nostrils of a grizzly? Then came some bear tales, bloody night raids at aromatic camps. You bet, right here in this backcountry.

Ernie just smiled and held to his sky-watching. Gradually the talk ebbed, and we joined in quiet reverie. I suspect

Ernie knew all along that the best story of this night was the night itself, out over the trickling Snake River and the dark ridge on the horizon. Alpine fir spiked the forest silhouette against a blue-gray sky. Fog rested lightly on the willow bot-

toms. Dark strips of cloud played against a crescent moon cocked at a jaunty angle. Sweet dreams.

There's style to Ernie Nunn. Anything needs doing, he's there. Chase down a horse. Superheat home fries with homemade salsa. Break out the hard stuff to ease the saddle sores. He rides tall and light and springy. In an endless downpour, when saturated leather chaps had the weight of armor, he kicked out of file and trotted alongside, with a dimpled smile like the promise of sunshine. But Ernie has his limitations. "I'm gonna make a real Montana red dog out of you," he kept telling me in that unvarnished western drawl of his, even as he boosted me into my saddle. Hah.

As in the Targhee, times have changed in the Bridger-Teton. I had spent hours listening to litanies of mismanagement in Bridger-Teton past—large, mindless clear-cuts in erosive or recalcitrant soils, where regeneration is slow and scraggly. And in the logging community of Dubois, Wyoming, I heard bitter resentment at the drift of Bridger-Teton present and future, a shrinking timber harvest threatening jobs in the forest and in the Louisiana-Pacific mill, which closed in the spring of 1988.

"What I see as the major change coming about," said Bridger-Teton Supervisor Brian Stout, "is the recognition that we're not a major timber-producing forest. We just simply

Skilled skiers plunge more than 15 feet into Corbet's Couloir (opposite) at Jackson Hole Ski Resort, a downhill mecca with more than a hundred miles of runs. The town of Jackson (above) offers entertainment around the clock— including dining and dancing after a night run down brightly lit slopes at Snow King Ski Resort.

FOLLOWING PAGES: Mist rings a hot spring at West Thumb Geyser Basin—a pocket of thermal springs, mud pots, and geysers on the shore of Yellowstone Lake.

aren't in the location and at the elevation and with the soil types where we can be a major contributor to America's need for wood fiber. What I think the public is telling us on this forest is that our proximity to the two national parks, the wilderness values and natural attractions we have on the forest—that one of the highest values we need to be managing for is recreation."

Across the ecosystem there are differences in missions between park and forest; the parks emphasize preservation, the forests manage for multiple use with conservation. There are also differences in logging policy among the forests. This was acknowledged in *The Greater Yellowstone Area*, published in 1987, a voluminous survey of existing resources and future management plans. Sponsored by a committee of forest and park executives, the study is seen as a step on the long road to fully coordinated planning for Yellowstone country.

Mid-November. Quiet time in Yellowstone Park. Roads closed. Ten inches of snow at Canyon; eighteen at Lewis Falls. A half inch at Mammoth Hot Springs on the northern edge, where steam rising and a ghostly hillside mark the terraces of travertine. This is the warmest region of the park. On nearby MacMinn Bench, a lofty sun porch, bighorn sheep were basking. Pronghorns shared the bench, their handsome palomino colors blending with the weathered grasses.

The mountain sheep were just beginning to rut. A handful of old rams clumped together in a rugby scrum, poking foreheads into one another's sides. While they were so occupied, young rams harried the ewes in the band, without encouragement. A big ram, dark brown and stocky, broke out of the clump and froze in a formal display of horn, a fine full curl. The other old rams kicked at each other for a bit, leg to flank. One charged, bumped into a backside. Where was the storied head-knocking? Perhaps it was too early in the season.

Soon the old boy network dissolved. Some grazed, others trotted down to the ewes. So went the November morning on sunny MacMinn Bench. A little scrimmaging, a little ewe chasing, limitless time out for nibbling. Not a bad life.

A month and a half later I observed a different group of bighorns. Just after New Year's Day the Wyoming Game and Fish Department spread apple squeezings (the solid dregs from cider presses, not the good stuff) on a patch of frozen ridge in the Wind River Range near Dubois. We were in the Whiskey Basin Habitat Unit, home of a thousand bighorns, one of the largest herds in the country.

*T*he apple dregs, in ferment, were warm and steamy, and the sheep loved the stuff. But there was a catch: It lay under a huge, pole-hung net. They piddled around the perimeter, sheepishly we'll say, then edged in. Never bet against gluttony. Biologist John Emmerich triggered a switch and plop!— down went the net. The bighorns bolted, bouncing up like popcorn, going nowhere. Workers and volunteers wrestled the panicky sheep down, as gently as we could, keeping a tight hold on the horns. The big ram horns can give you a headache; the spikes of the ewes and young rams can impale an eye. We and the sheep—those big reproachful eyes staring— toughed it out through inoculations, tagging, weighing. Then into waiting trucks they went.

"Wonderful," beamed Dick Baldes. "We're making history today." Dick was a U.S. Fish and Wildlife Service biologist, serving the Shoshone and Arapaho on the Wind River Indian

Bison and snowmobilers come to terms on the Hayden Valley road. In winter, roads carry almost 900 snowmobiles a day, as well as animals that leave drifted fields for easier travel on snow-packed surfaces. Rangers ask drivers to yield the right-of-way to wildlife, but collisions do occur. The coyote below, probably struck by a snowmobile, was so badly injured it had to be destroyed.

FOLLOWING PAGES: Squad of snowmobilers roars down a snowy road in Yellowstone Park. Though they shatter the frozen stillness, snowmobiles make winter patrols and rescues possible. To limit noise and protect wildlife, the park sets top speed at 45 miles an hour.

Cross-country skier skims across Virginia Meadows along the Gibbon River.

Growing numbers of skiers delight in Yellowstone's blanketed backcountry.

Reservation. A Shoshone himself, Dick had struggled through harsh years—bullet holes in his camper, intertribal hostility—to end unregulated hunting on the reservation. In time a game code was established; wildlife increased. As a gesture of support for the conservation effort, Wyoming donated some 50 bighorns to the reservation that day and has since donated 41 animals in 1993 and another 43 in 1995.

Trucks pulling laden trailers rolled down the southeast leg of the ecosystem, beside the icy Wind River Range, through the reservation to the canyon of the South Fork of the Little Wind River. The doors opened, and soon the bighorns burst out and flew up the canyon walls. Two got hung up in a willow tangle in leaping stance, all fours off the ground; I thought of the image in Genesis, during the testing of Abraham: "and behold behind *him* a ram caught in a thicket by his horns. . . ." But these two were not sacrificial sheep; they thrashed through the willows and were gone.

Dick Baldes loves to make history. Last time we talked he was dreaming of bringing the wolf back—an issue mired in some real and some fairy-tale fears elsewhere in Yellowstone country. On the 2.2-million-acre Indian reservation, Dick explained, all it would take is approval by the two tribal councils.

From bighorn country I swung back north to Jackson Hole, well into the skiing season now—downhill at three nearby areas (two in Bridger-Teton National Forest, one in the Targhee), cross-country all over. For the wild ones, those who seek "virgin descents," there's untracked terrain up around Teton Pass; for the tamer crowd, there's the flat along Cottonwood Creek in Grand Teton Park.

The National Elk Refuge has the valley's biggest crowd of winter visitors, up to 30,000, triple the number of visitors in 1988. The animals loll on the frozen ground or nibble at the grasses poking up through the thin, patchy snow. When the snow gets thick and crusty, the refuge will spread alfalfa pellets.

A few coyotes patrol the periphery of the elk clusters. Thin snow is good news for coyotes too; they don't have to dig deep for mice. When an elk dies, the coyotes join the scavengers' ball—ravens, magpies, bald eagles, occasionally a golden eagle.

All through the winter huge wagons with sled runners, pulled by Clydesdales and Belgians and shires, take visitors out for a close look at the elk. The ride is bumpy and cold and exhilarating—a living Christmas card. No winter should be without elk and big sleighs and beer-wagon horses, and the Tetons for a backdrop.

A few days after the sleigh ride in Jackson Hole, I took a longer, much bumpier ride in a wheezy, noisy old snow machine, its innards fumy and foggy. It is called a snowcoach—and many other things by drivers who steer, wipe windows, troubleshoot, and keep up a steady patter about the passing scene. The paying passengers willingly tolerate the ordeal, for it is their rite of passage into the otherworld of Yellowstone Park in winter.

Until the 1970s the frozen park was largely a secret world. Now the wonderland has been discovered. Some 120,000 visitors penetrate it each winter, by automobile from the north, by snowcoach from north, south, and west, by snowmobiles from nearly all sides. Off the roads, away from the roar, the way to go is on cross-country skis. Ski to the geysers, ski to wildlife, ski to blue-ice bergs and cataracts. Unreal country. Addictive.

"It's more than an addiction," said Ed Greenwood. "This is our sanctuary." He and Jane Furze of Phoenix, Arizona, had just arrived at the Old Faithful Visitor Center for their sixth winter visit. To me it looked like a homecoming, with warm greetings, family chatter, gifts. What's new? Any change in Old Faithful? How are Beehive and Giant and Grand?

There were packages. "I've noticed," said Jane, "that rangers develop a certain craving, and Ed's mom's trees were loaded." She unwrapped a bentwood basket, the pickings resting on gift-box straw. Citrus, avocados. Naturalist Sandy Snell's eyes popped. "Oh, look at that!" As soon as the visitor traffic thinned she headed for a back room and started peeling grapefruit. Winter naturalists don't see much of that.

Outside, the winds were boxing the compass. The steam from Old Faithful and its neighbors on Geyser Hill swirled now one way, now another. When Old Faithful erupted, the water flagged out to the east. Then the wind dropped and the discharge billowed up into a mushroom. A three-swan V winged around the geyser—the birds' necks stretched taut, not the graceful arcs of floating swans. In a few moments the white trumpeters blended into the gray sky.

Jen Hutchinson, who lives here winter and summer, once saw a flight of Canada geese go over Giantess Geyser just as it erupted. "They suddenly backpedaled furiously, as if stunned, trying to get out of the way," she recalled as we toured Geyser Hill. Jen, a botanist, picked out the small winter wonders of this "thermal hothouse"—green leaves of monkey flowers beside a warm seep; Panicum, or panic grass; and the tiny, thin leaves of the endemic known as Ross bent grass, which grows in the Upper, Midway, and Lower Geyser Basins and has been found nowhere else in the world.

Photographer focuses from the open roof of a snowcoach (opposite)— a tracked vehicle that transports visitors through the snowbound park.

FOLLOWING PAGES: Competing with clouds, a plume of water and mist jets 75 feet from Riverside Geyser, arching across the Firehole River in Upper Geyser Basin. The two-square-mile basin, reached by trail from the Grand Loop, holds the largest concentration of geysers in the world. Riverside, one of the most reliable, erupts about every seven hours.

*T*he bison on the slopes of Geyser Hill had grown good winter coats, full and thick; gone were the tattered hobo coats of summer. There were geese on the dark ribbon of the Firehole River. Jen's husband, Rick, the thermal specialist at Old Faithful, told me the heat that goes into the Firehole can melt seven tons of ice per minute. Elsewhere in the park the rainbow trout breed in spring, when the spawning waters warm to 50°F. In the Firehole the rainbows spawn around Christmas, when the water cools to 50 degrees.

Skiing Geyser Hill is an adventure in self-discovery. What I discovered, or rather rediscovered, is that I do not know how to ski. Descending to the bridge over the (Continued on page 190)

*S*erene adult trumpeter swans sail the snow-banked Madison River. Many trumpeters migrate from Canada to winter near the park's thermal waters; others reside here all year. The birds guard nesting territory with trumpeting cries and raised wings that span eight feet.

FOLLOWING PAGES: *Silhouettes in the mist, bison search for food in Midway Geyser Basin. Area thermal springs warm the ground and melt snow cover, making grasses and sedges more accessible than elsewhere in the frozen park. The springs also discharge hot water into the nearby Firehole River, where elk and other animals find nourishment even in winter.*